BAKING

ESSENTIAL RECIPES FOR THE BEST
COOKIES, CAKES, PIES & BREADS

Publications International, Ltd.

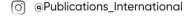

Let's get social!

@Publications_International

@PublicationsInternational

www.pilcookbooks.com

CONTENTS

Cakes 4

Pies & Tarts 36

Breads..64

Cookies 96

Bar Cookies 128

Desserts...160

Index..188

CAKES

Pumpkin Streusel Coffeecake

MAKES 9 SERVINGS

STREUSEL

- ½ **cup all-purpose flour**
- ½ **cup packed brown sugar**
- 2 **teaspoons ground cinnamon**
- ¼ **cup (½ stick) butter, softened**
- ½ **cup chopped walnuts**

COFFEECAKE

- 2 **cups all-purpose flour**
- 2 **teaspoons baking powder**
- ¾ **teaspoon pumpkin pie spice**
- ½ **teaspoon baking soda**
- ½ **teaspoon salt**
- ¾ **cup packed brown sugar**
- ½ **cup (1 stick) butter, softened**
- 2 **eggs**
- 1 **cup canned pumpkin**
- 2 **teaspoons vanilla**

1. Preheat oven to 325°F. Spray 8-inch square baking pan with nonstick cooking spray.

2. For streusel, combine ½ cup flour, ½ cup brown sugar and cinnamon in small bowl; mix well. Cut in ¼ cup butter with pastry blender or mix with fingers until coarse crumbs form. Stir in walnuts. Refrigerate until ready to use.

3. For coffeecake, combine 2 cups flour, baking powder, pumpkin pie spice, baking soda and salt in medium bowl; mix well. Beat ¾ cup brown sugar and ½ cup butter in large bowl with electric mixer at medium-high speed until light and fluffy. Add eggs, one at a time, beating well at medium speed after each addition. Beat in pumpkin and vanilla until well blended. Add flour mixture; beat at low speed until blended. (Batter will be very thick.) Spread half of batter in prepared baking pan; sprinkle with half of streusel. Top with remaining batter and streusel.

4. Bake about 40 minutes or until toothpick inserted into center comes out clean. Cool completely in pan on wire rack.

Classic Chocolate Birthday Cake

MAKES 12 SERVINGS

2 cups all-purpose flour

3$\frac{1}{4}$ cups sugar, divided

$\frac{2}{3}$ cup unsweetened cocoa powder

2 teaspoons baking soda

1$\frac{1}{2}$ teaspoons baking powder

$\frac{3}{4}$ teaspoon salt

1$\frac{3}{4}$ cups buttermilk

$\frac{1}{2}$ cup vegetable oil

2 eggs

2 teaspoons vanilla, divided

6 ounces unsweetened chocolate, chopped

$\frac{1}{2}$ cup (1 stick) butter, cut into pieces

1 cup whipping cream

1. Preheat oven to 350°F. Line bottoms of two 9-inch cake pans with parchment paper; spray pans and paper with nonstick cooking spray.

2. Combine flour, 1$\frac{3}{4}$ cups sugar, cocoa, baking soda, baking powder and salt in large bowl; mix well. Whisk buttermilk, oil, eggs and 1 teaspoon vanilla in medium bowl until blended. Stir into flour mixture until well blended. Pour batter into prepared pans.

3. Bake 22 to 24 minutes or until toothpick inserted into centers comes out clean. Cool in pans 10 minutes; remove to wire racks to cool completely.

4. Combine chocolate and butter in medium bowl. Heat remaining 1$\frac{1}{2}$ cups sugar and cream in small saucepan over medium-high heat, stirring until sugar is dissolved. When cream begins to bubble, reduce heat to low; simmer 5 minutes. Pour over chocolate mixture; stir until smooth. Stir in remaining 1 teaspoon vanilla. Refrigerate until frosting is cool and thickened, stirring occasionally.

5. Place one cake layer on serving plate; spread with 1 cup frosting. Top with second cake layer; frost top and side of cake with remaining frosting. Refrigerate at least 1 hour before slicing.

Oat Apricot Snack Cake

MAKES 24 SERVINGS

1 container (6 ounces) plain yogurt (not fat free)

¾ cup packed brown sugar

½ cup granulated sugar

⅓ cup vegetable oil

1 egg

2 tablespoons milk

2 teaspoons vanilla

1 cup all-purpose flour

½ cup whole wheat flour

1 teaspoon baking soda

1 teaspoon ground cinnamon

½ teaspoon salt

2 cups old-fashioned oats

1 cup (about 6 ounces) chopped dried apricots

2 tablespoons milk

1 cup powdered sugar

1. Preheat oven to 350°F. Spray 13×9-inch baking pan with nonstick cooking spray.

2. Whisk yogurt, brown sugar, granulated sugar, oil, egg, milk and vanilla in large bowl until well blended. Sift all-purpose flour, whole wheat flour, baking soda, cinnamon and salt into medium bowl. Add to yogurt mixture; stir until blended. Stir in oats and apricots until well blended. Spread batter in prepared pan.

3. Bake 25 to 30 minutes or until toothpick inserted into center comes out clean. Cool completely in pan on wire rack.

4. Stir milk into powdered sugar in small bowl until smooth. Spoon glaze into small resealable food storage bag; seal bag. Cut ¼ inch from one corner; drizzle glaze over cake.

Turtle Cheesecake

MAKES 12 SERVINGS

CRUST

- ½ cup (1 stick) butter
- 4 ounces semisweet baking chocolate, chopped
- ½ cup sugar
- 2 eggs
- ½ teaspoon salt
- ½ teaspoon vanilla
- ¾ cup all-purpose flour
- ½ cup finely chopped pecans

FILLING

- 4 packages (8 ounces each) cream cheese, softened
- 1 cup sugar
- 1½ teaspoons vanilla
- ½ cup sour cream
- 4 eggs
- ½ cup caramel ice cream topping

TOPPING

- ½ cup chopped pecans
- 2 tablespoons caramel ice cream topping

GARNISH

- 1 cup prepared fudge frosting

1. Preheat oven to 350°F. Spray 9-inch springform pan with nonstick cooking spray. Wrap outside of pan with foil.

2. For crust, melt butter and chocolate in medium saucepan over low heat, stirring frequently until smooth. Remove from heat; stir in ½ cup sugar until blended. Add 2 eggs, one at a time, stirring until well blended after each addition. Stir in salt and ½ teaspoon vanilla. Stir in flour and ½ cup pecans just until blended. Spread evenly in prepared pan. Bake 15 minutes or until top is set but still soft. Remove from oven and place in larger baking pan.

3. For filling, beat cream cheese in large bowl with electric mixer at low speed until creamy. Add 1 cup sugar and 1½ teaspoons vanilla; beat until well blended. Add sour cream; beat until blended. With mixer running at medium speed, add 4 eggs, one at a time, beating until well blended after each addition. Spread half of filling over crust. Drop ¼ cup caramel topping by teaspoonfuls over filling; swirl with skewer or knife. Top with remaining filling. Drop remaining ¼ cup caramel topping by teaspoonfuls over filling; swirl with skewer. Place pan in oven; add hot water to larger pan to come halfway up side of springform pan.

4. Bake 1 hour or until top of cheesecake is almost set. Immediately run knife around side of cheesecake to loosen. Cool completely in pan on wire rack. Refrigerate 4 hours or overnight.

5. For topping, cook and stir $1/2$ cup pecans in small skillet over medium-low heat 3 to 5 minutes or until fragrant and lightly browned. Add 2 tablespoons caramel topping; cook 1 minute or until nuts are glazed. Spread over top of cheesecake.

6. Place frosting in piping bag or large resealable food storage bag fitted with large star tip. Pipe rosettes around edge of cheesecake.

Angel Food Cake

MAKES 10 TO 12 SERVINGS

1¼ **cups cake flour, sifted**

1⅓ **cups plus ½ cup sugar, divided**

12 **egg whites**

1¼ **teaspoons cream of tartar**

1½ **teaspoons vanilla**

¼ **teaspoon salt**

Fresh strawberries (optional)

1. Preheat oven to 350°F.

2. Sift flour and ½ cup sugar into medium bowl.

3. Beat egg whites, cream of tartar, vanilla and salt in large bowl with electric mixer at high speed until soft peaks form. Gradually add remaining 1⅓ cups sugar, beating until stiff peaks form. Fold in flour mixture. Pour batter into *ungreased* 10-inch tube pan.

4. Bake 35 to 40 minutes or until cake springs back when lightly touched.

5. Invert pan; place on top of clean empty bottle. Let cake cool completely in pan upside down. Invert cake onto serving plate. Serve with strawberries, if desired.

Butterscotch Malt Zucchini Cake

MAKES 10 TO 12 SERVINGS

1¾ cups packed brown sugar

½ cup (1 stick) butter

½ cup vegetable oil

2 eggs

½ cup buttermilk

1 teaspoon vanilla

2½ cups all-purpose flour

4 tablespoons malted milk powder

1 teaspoon baking soda

½ teaspoon salt

½ teaspoon baking powder

½ teaspoon ground nutmeg

2 cups grated zucchini

¾ cup white chocolate chips, divided

¾ cup butterscotch chips, divided

½ cup chopped nuts

1. Preheat oven to 350°F. Grease and flour 12-cup (10-inch) bundt pan.

2. Beat brown sugar, butter, oil and eggs in large bowl with electric mixer at medium speed 2 minutes. Add buttermilk and vanilla; beat until well blended.

3. Combine flour, malted milk powder, baking soda, salt, baking powder and nutmeg in medium bowl; mix well. Stir into butter mixture just until blended. Stir in zucchini, ½ cup white chocolate chips, ½ cup butterscotch chips and chopped nuts. Pour batter into prepared pan.

4. Bake 60 to 65 minutes or until toothpick inserted near center comes out clean. Cool completely on wire rack.

5. Place remaining ¼ cup white chocolate chips in small microwavable bowl; microwave on HIGH 30 seconds. Stir; microwave in 10-second intervals until melted and smooth, stirring after each interval. Drizzle over cake. Repeat melting process with remaining ¼ cup butterscotch chips; drizzle over cake.

Chocolate Sheet Cake

MAKES 12 TO 16 SERVINGS

CAKE

- 1½ **cups granulated sugar**
- 1¾ **cups all-purpose flour**
- ¾ **cup unsweetened cocoa powder**
- ½ **cup packed brown sugar**
- 1½ **teaspoons baking soda**
- 1½ **teaspoons baking powder**
- 1 **teaspoon salt**
- 1 **cup buttermilk or milk**
- 2 **eggs, lightly beaten**
- ½ **cup vegetable oil**
- 1 **teaspoon vanilla**
- 2 **teaspoons instant coffee granules or instant espresso powder**
- 1 **cup boiling water**

FROSTING

- 1 **can (15 ounces) sweet potato purée**
- **Pinch salt**
- 1 **package (10 ounces) bittersweet or semisweet chocolate chips**
- ½ **teaspoon vanilla**
- **Colored decors (optional)**

1. Preheat oven to 350°F. Spray 13×9-inch baking pan with nonstick cooking spray.

2. For cake, combine granulated sugar, flour, cocoa, brown sugar, baking soda, baking powder and 1 teaspoon salt in large bowl of electric stand mixer; beat at low speed to blend. Add buttermilk, eggs, oil and 1 teaspoon vanilla; beat at medium speed 2 minutes.

3. Stir coffee granules into boiling water in measuring cup or small bowl until well blended. Add to chocolate mixture; stir until blended. (Batter will be thin.) Pour batter into prepared pan.

4. Bake about 30 minutes or until toothpick inserted into center comes out clean. Cool completely in pan on wire rack.

5. For frosting, combine sweet potato purée and pinch of salt in large saucepan; bring to a simmer over medium heat, stirring frequently. Remove from heat; stir in chocolate and ½ teaspoon vanilla until melted and smooth. Let frosting stand until thickened and cooled to room temperature, stirring occasionally.

6. Spread frosting over cake; top with decors, if desired.

Red Velvet Cake

MAKES 10 TO 12 SERVINGS

CAKE

- 2 cups all-purpose flour
- 2 tablespoons unsweetened cocoa powder
- 1 teaspoon salt
- 1¼ cups buttermilk
- 1 bottle (1 ounce) red food coloring
- 1 teaspoon vanilla
- 1½ cups granulated sugar
- 1 cup (2 sticks) butter, softened
- 2 eggs
- 1 tablespoon white or cider vinegar
- 1½ teaspoons baking soda

FROSTING

- 2 packages (8 ounces each) cream cheese, softened
- ½ cup (1 stick) butter, softened
- 6 cups powdered sugar
- ¼ cup milk
- 2 teaspoons vanilla
- 4 ounces white chocolate, shaved with vegetable peeler

1. Preheat oven to 350°F. Spray three 9-inch cake pans with nonstick cooking spray. Line bottoms of pans with parchment paper; spray paper with cooking spray.

2. For cake, combine flour, cocoa and salt in medium bowl. Combine buttermilk, food coloring and vanilla in small bowl; mix well.

3. Beat granulated sugar and 1 cup butter in large bowl with electric mixer at medium speed 5 minutes or until light and fluffy. Add eggs, one at a time, beating until well blended after each addition. Add flour mixture alternately with buttermilk mixture, beating at low speed after each addition. Stir vinegar into baking soda in small bowl. Add to batter; stir gently until blended. Pour batter into prepared pans.

4. Bake about 20 minutes or until toothpick inserted into centers comes out clean. Cool in pans 10 minutes. Invert onto wire racks; peel off parchment. Cool completely.

5. For frosting, beat cream cheese and ½ cup butter in large bowl with electric mixer at medium speed until creamy. Add powdered sugar, milk and 2 teaspoons vanilla; beat at low speed until blended. Beat at medium speed until smooth.

6. Place one cake layer on serving plate; spread with 1½ cups frosting. Top with second cake layer; spread with 1½ cups frosting. Top with remaining cake layer; spread remaining frosting over top and side of cake. Press white chocolate shavings onto side of cake.

Toffee Cake with Whiskey Sauce

MAKES 9 SERVINGS

8 ounces chopped dates

2$1/4$ teaspoons baking soda, divided

1$1/2$ cups boiling water

2 cups all-purpose flour

$1/2$ teaspoon salt

$3/4$ cup (1$1/2$ sticks) butter, softened

$1/2$ cup granulated sugar

$1/2$ cup packed dark brown sugar

2 eggs

1 teaspoon vanilla

1$1/2$ cups butterscotch ice cream topping

2 tablespoons whiskey

1 cup glazed pecans* or chopped toasted pecans

Vanilla ice cream

Glazed pecans can be found in the produce section of many supermarkets with other salad toppings.

1. Preheat oven to 350°F. Spray 9-inch square baking pan with nonstick cooking spray.

2. Combine dates and 1$1/2$ teaspoons baking soda in medium bowl. Stir in boiling water; let stand 10 minutes to soften. Mash with fork or process in food processor until mixture forms paste.

3. Combine flour, remaining $3/4$ teaspoon baking soda and salt in medium bowl; mix well. Beat butter, granulated sugar and brown sugar in large bowl with electric mixer at medium speed 3 minutes or until creamy. Add eggs, one at a time, beating until well blended after each addition. Beat in vanilla. Add flour mixture alternately with date mixture; beat at low speed just until blended. Spread batter in prepared pan.

4. Bake about 30 minutes or until toothpick inserted into center comes out with moist crumbs. Cool in pan on wire rack 15 minutes.

5. Heat butterscotch topping in medium microwavable bowl on HIGH 30 seconds or until warm; stir in whiskey. Drizzle sauce over each serving; sprinkle with pecans and top with ice cream.

Glazed Applesauce Spice Cake

MAKES 12 SERVINGS

1 **cup packed brown sugar**

³/₄ **cup (1¹/₂ sticks) butter, softened**

3 **eggs**

1¹/₂ **teaspoons vanilla**

2¹/₄ **cups all-purpose flour**

2 **teaspoons baking soda**

2 **teaspoons ground cinnamon**

³/₄ **teaspoon ground nutmeg**

¹/₂ **teaspoon ground ginger**

¹/₄ **teaspoon salt**

1¹/₂ **cups unsweetened applesauce**

¹/₂ **cup milk**

²/₃ **cup chopped walnuts**

²/₃ **cup butterscotch chips**

Apple Glaze (recipe follows)

1. Preheat oven to 350°F. Grease and lightly flour 12-cup bundt pan or 10-inch tube pan.

2. Beat brown sugar and butter in large bowl with electric mixer at medium speed until light and fluffy. Beat in eggs and vanilla until well blended. Combine flour, baking soda, cinnamon, nutmeg, ginger and salt in medium bowl; mix well. Add to butter mixture alternately with applesauce and milk, beginning and ending with flour mixture, beating well after each addition. Stir in walnuts and butterscotch chips. Pour batter into prepared pan.

3. Bake 45 to 50 minutes or until toothpick inserted near center comes out clean. Cool in pan 15 minutes; invert onto wire rack to cool completely.

4. Prepare Apple Glaze; spoon over top of cake.

APPLE GLAZE: Place 1 cup sifted powdered sugar in small bowl. Stir in 2 to 3 tablespoons apple juice concentrate to make stiff glaze.

Blueberry Crumb Cake

MAKES 12 TO 15 SERVINGS

Crumb Topping (recipe follows)

2 cups all-purpose flour

²/₃ cup sugar

1 tablespoon baking powder

1 teaspoon salt

½ teaspoon baking soda

1 cup milk

½ cup (1 stick) butter, melted

2 eggs

2 tablespoons lemon juice

2 cups fresh or thawed frozen blueberries

1. Preheat oven to 375°F. Spray 13×9-inch baking pan with nonstick cooking spray. Prepare Crumb Topping.

2. Sift flour, sugar, baking powder, salt and baking soda into large bowl. Whisk milk, butter, eggs and lemon juice in medium bowl until well blended. Pour into flour mixture; stir until blended. Pour batter into prepared pan.

3. Sprinkle blueberries evenly over batter; sprinkle with Crumb Topping.

4. Bake 40 to 45 minutes or until toothpick inserted into center comes out clean. Serve warm.

CRUMB TOPPING: Combine 1 cup chopped walnuts or pecans, ²/₃ cup sugar, ½ cup all-purpose flour, ¼ cup (½ stick) softened butter and ½ teaspoon ground cinnamon in large bowl until mixture forms coarse crumbs.

cakes | # Carrot Cake
MAKES 8 TO 10 SERVINGS

CAKE

- 2 **cups all-purpose flour**
- 2 **teaspoons baking soda**
- 2 **teaspoons ground cinnamon**
- 1 **teaspoon salt**
- 4 **eggs**
- 2¼ **cups granulated sugar**
- 1 **cup vegetable oil**
- 1 **cup buttermilk**
- 1 **tablespoon vanilla**
- 3 **medium carrots, shredded (3 cups)**
- 3 **cups walnuts, chopped and toasted,* divided**
- 1 **cup shredded coconut**
- 1 **can (8 ounces) crushed pineapple**

FROSTING

- 2 **packages (8 ounces each) cream cheese, softened**
- 1 **cup (2 sticks) butter, softened**
  Pinch salt
- 3 **cups powdered sugar**
- 1 **tablespoon orange juice**
- 2 **teaspoons grated orange peel**
- 1 **teaspoon vanilla**

*To toast walnuts, spread on ungreased baking sheet. Bake in preheated 350°F oven 6 to 8 minutes or until lightly browned, stirring frequently.

1. Preheat oven to 350°F. Spray two 9-inch round cake pans with nonstick cooking spray. Line bottoms of pans with parchment paper; spray paper with cooking spray.

2. For cake, combine flour, baking soda, cinnamon and 1 teaspoon salt in medium bowl; mix well. Whisk eggs in large bowl until blended. Add granulated sugar, oil, buttermilk and 1 tablespoon vanilla; whisk until well blended. Add flour mixture; stir until well blended. Add carrots, 1 cup walnuts, coconut and pineapple; stir just until blended. Pour batter into prepared pans.

3. Bake 25 to 30 minutes or until toothpick inserted into centers comes out clean. Cool in pans 10 minutes; remove to wire racks to cool completely.

4. For frosting, beat cream cheese, butter and pinch of salt in large bowl with electric mixer at medium speed 3 minutes or until creamy. Add powdered sugar, orange juice, orange peel and 1 teaspoon vanilla; beat at low speed until blended. Beat at medium speed 2 minutes or until frosting is smooth.

5. Place one cake layer on serving plate; spread with 2 cups frosting. Top with second cake layer; frost top and side of cake with remaining frosting. Press 1¾ cups walnuts onto side of cake. Sprinkle remaining ¼ cup walnuts over top of cake.

Pumpkin Cheesecake
MAKES 12 SERVINGS

CRUST

- 18 graham crackers (2 sleeves)
- ¼ cup sugar
- ⅛ teaspoon salt
- ½ cup (1 stick) butter, melted

FILLING

- 1 can (15 ounces) solid-pack pumpkin
- ¼ cup sour cream
- 2 teaspoons vanilla
- 2 teaspoons ground cinnamon, plus additional for garnish
- 1 teaspoon ground ginger
- ¼ teaspoon salt
- ¼ teaspoon ground cloves
- 4 packages (8 ounces each) cream cheese, softened
- 1¾ cups sugar
- 5 eggs
  Whipped cream

1. Line bottom of 9-inch springform with parchment paper. Spray bottom and side of pan with nonstick cooking spray. Wrap outside of pan with heavy-duty foil.

2. For crust, place graham crackers in food processor; pulse until fine crumbs form. Add ¼ cup sugar and ⅛ teaspoon salt; pulse to blend. Add butter; pulse until crumbs are moistened and mixture is well blended. Press crumb mixture onto bottom and all the way up side of prepared pan in thin layer. Refrigerate at least 20 minutes.

3. Preheat oven to 350°F. Bake crust 12 minutes; cool on wire rack.

4. For filling, whisk pumpkin, sour cream, vanilla, 2 teaspoons cinnamon, ginger, ¼ teaspoon salt and cloves in medium bowl until well blended. Beat cream cheese and 1¾ cups sugar in large bowl with electric mixer at medium speed until smooth and well blended. With mixer running, beat in eggs, one at a time, until blended. Scrape side of bowl. Add pumpkin mixture; beat at medium speed until well blended. Pour into crust. Place springform pan in large roasting pan; place in oven. Carefully add boiling water to roasting pan to come about halfway up side of springform pan.

5. Bake 1 hour 15 minutes or until top is set and lightly browned but still jiggly. Remove cheesecake from water; remove foil. Cool to room temperature on wire rack. Run small thin spatula around edge of pan to loosen crust. (Do not remove side of pan.)

6. Cover with plastic wrap and refrigerate 8 hours or overnight. Garnish with whipped cream and additional cinnamon.

Peanut Butter Cupcakes

MAKES 24 CUPCAKES

1 cup creamy peanut butter, divided

¼ cup (½ stick) butter, softened

1 cup packed brown sugar

2 eggs

2 cups all-purpose flour

2 teaspoons baking powder

½ teaspoon baking soda

½ teaspoon salt

1 cup milk

1½ cups mini semisweet chocolate chips, divided, plus additional for garnish

Peanut Buttery Frosting (recipe follows)

1. Preheat oven to 350°F. Line 24 standard (2½-inch) muffin cups with paper baking cups.

2. Beat ½ cup peanut butter and butter in large bowl with electric mixer at medium speed until blended. Add brown sugar; beat until well blended. Add eggs, one at a time, beating well after each addition.

3. Combine flour, baking powder, baking soda and salt in small bowl; mix well. Add to peanut butter mixture alternately with milk; beat at low speed until blended. Stir in 1 cup chocolate chips. Spoon batter evenly into prepared muffin cups.

4. Bake 15 minutes or until toothpick inserted into centers comes out clean. (Cover with foil if tops of cupcakes begin to brown too much.) Cool completely in pans on wire racks. Meanwhile, prepare Peanut Buttery Frosting.

5. Pipe or spread frosting on cupcakes. Place remaining ½ cup peanut butter in small microwavable bowl. Microwave on HIGH 15 seconds or until melted. Place remaining ½ cup chocolate chips in another small microwavable bowl. Microwave on HIGH 15 seconds or until melted. Drizzle melted peanut butter and chocolate over frosting. Garnish with additional chocolate chips.

PEANUT BUTTERY FROSTING: Beat ½ cup (1 stick) softened butter and ½ cup creamy peanut butter in large bowl with electric mixer at medium speed until smooth. Gradually beat in 2 cups sifted powdered sugar and ½ teaspoon vanilla until blended. Add 3 to 6 tablespoons milk, 1 tablespoon at a time, until smooth.

Pear Spice Cake

MAKES 12 SERVINGS

4 cups chopped peeled pears

2 cups granulated sugar

1 cup chopped walnuts

3 cups all-purpose flour

2 teaspoons baking soda

3/4 teaspoon ground cinnamon

1/2 teaspoon salt

1/4 teaspoon ground nutmeg

1/8 teaspoon ground cloves

1 cup vegetable oil

2 eggs

1 1/2 teaspoons vanilla

Powdered sugar (optional)

1. Combine pears, granulated sugar and walnuts in medium bowl; mix gently. Let stand 1 hour, stirring occasionally.

2. Preheat oven to 375°F. Grease and flour 12-cup bundt pan or 10-inch tube pan.

3. Combine flour, baking soda, cinnamon, salt, nutmeg and cloves in medium bowl; mix well. Beat oil, eggs and vanilla in large bowl until well blended. Add flour mixture; stir until blended. Stir in pear mixture until blended. Pour batter into prepared pan.

4. Bake 1 hour 10 minutes or until toothpick inserted near center comes out clean. Cool in pan 20 minutes. Loosen edges of cake; invert onto wire rack to cool completely.

5. Sprinkle lightly with powdered sugar, if desired.

Banana Cake

MAKES 12 TO 16 SERVINGS

2½ **cups all-purpose flour**

1 **tablespoon baking soda**

½ **teaspoon salt**

1 **cup granulated sugar**

¾ **cup packed brown sugar**

½ **cup (1 stick) butter, softened**

2 **eggs**

1 **teaspoon vanilla**

3 **ripe bananas, mashed (about 1⅔ cups)**

⅔ **cup buttermilk**

1 **container (16 ounces) dark chocolate frosting***

*Or use recipe for chocolate frosting on page 16 instead of using prepared frosting.

1. Preheat oven to 350°F. Spray two 8-inch round cake pans with nonstick cooking spray.

2. Combine flour, baking soda and salt in medium bowl; mix well. Beat granulated sugar, brown sugar and butter in large bowl with electric mixer at medium speed until well blended. Add eggs and vanilla; beat until blended. Stir in bananas. Alternately add flour mixture and buttermilk; beat at low speed until blended. Pour batter into prepared pans.

3. Bake 35 minutes or until toothpick inserted into centers comes out clean. Cool in pans 10 minutes; remove to wire racks to cool completely.

4. Fill and frost cake with chocolate frosting.

PIES & TARTS

Sweet Potato Pecan Pie

MAKES 8 SERVINGS

1 sweet potato
   (about 1 pound)

3 eggs, divided

8 tablespoons granulated
   sugar, divided

8 tablespoons packed brown
   sugar, divided

2 tablespoons butter, melted,
   divided

½ teaspoon ground cinnamon

½ teaspoon salt, divided

1 frozen 9-inch deep-dish
   pie crust

½ cup dark corn syrup

1½ teaspoons lemon juice

1½ teaspoons vanilla

1 cup pecan halves

   Vanilla ice cream (optional)

1. Preheat oven to 350°F. Prick sweet potato all over with fork. Bake 1 hour or until fork-tender; let stand until cool enough to handle. Peel sweet potato and place in bowl of electric stand mixer. *Reduce oven temperature to 300°F.*

2. Add 1 egg, 2 tablespoons granulated sugar, 2 tablespoons brown sugar, 1 tablespoon butter, cinnamon and ¼ teaspoon salt to bowl with sweet potato; beat at medium speed 5 minutes or until smooth and fluffy. Spread mixture in frozen crust; place in refrigerator.

3. Combine corn syrup, remaining 6 tablespoons granulated sugar, 6 tablespoons brown sugar, 1 tablespoon butter, lemon juice vanilla and remaining ¼ teaspoon salt in clean mixer bowl; beat at medium speed 5 minutes. Add remaining 2 eggs; beat 5 minutes. Place crust on baking sheet. Spread pecans over sweet potato filling; pour corn syrup mixture evenly over pecans.

4. Bake 1 hour or until center is set and top is deep golden brown. Cool completely. Serve with ice cream, if desired.

Bittersweet Chocolate Tarts

MAKES 10 TARTS

¾ **cup whipping cream**

1½ **cups bittersweet chocolate chips *or* 8 ounces bittersweet chocolate, chopped**

1½ **cups graham cracker crumbs**

6 **tablespoons (¾ stick) butter, melted**

⅓ **cup sugar**

Sweetened whipped cream (optional)

1. Heat cream to a simmer in microwave or on stovetop. Place chocolate in medium bowl; pour hot cream over chocolate. Let stand 1 minute; stir until smooth. Set filling aside to thicken while preparing tart crusts.

2. Preheat oven to 350°F. Spray 10 (3-inch) nonstick tart pans with nonstick cooking spray or line 10 standard (2½-inch) muffin cups with paper baking cups.

3. Combine graham cracker crumbs, butter and sugar in medium bowl; mix well. Press 2½ tablespoons crumb mixture into each prepared tart pan. (If using muffin cups, press crumb mixture evenly onto bottoms and two thirds up sides of cups.)

4. Bake about 8 minutes or until lightly browned. Cool completely in pans on wire rack or refrigerate 15 minutes to speed up cooling time.

5. To remove crusts from pans, invert tart pans onto plate, one at a time. Tap bottom of pan firmly with hand to release crust from pan. (If using muffin pan, remove paper baking cups from pan; peel off paper cups from crusts.)

6. Spread 2 tablespoons chocolate filling in each crust. Serve tarts with whipped cream, if desired.

Rustic Cranberry-Pear Galette

MAKES 8 SERVINGS

¼ cup sugar, divided

1 tablespoon plus 1 teaspoon cornstarch

2 teaspoons ground cinnamon or apple pie spice

4 cups thinly sliced peeled Bartlett pears

¼ cup dried cranberries

1 teaspoon vanilla

¼ teaspoon almond extract (optional)

1 refrigerated pie crust, at room temperature (half of 15-ounce package)

1 egg white

1 tablespoon water

1. Preheat oven to 450°F. Line baking sheet or pizza pan with parchment paper or spray with nonstick cooking spray.

2. Reserve 1 teaspoon sugar. Combine remaining sugar, cornstarch and cinnamon in medium bowl; mix well. Add pears, cranberries, vanilla and almond extract, if desired; toss to coat.

3. Place crust on prepared pan. Spoon pear mixture into center of crust, spreading to within 2 inches of edge. Fold edge of crust 2 inches over pear mixture, overlapping or pleating as necessary.

4. Whisk egg white and water in small bowl until well blended. Brush over crust; sprinkle with reserved 1 teaspoon sugar.

5. Bake 25 minutes or until pears are tender and crust is golden brown.* Cool on baking sheet on wire rack 30 minutes. Serve warm.

If edge browns too quickly, cover loosely with foil after 15 minutes of baking.

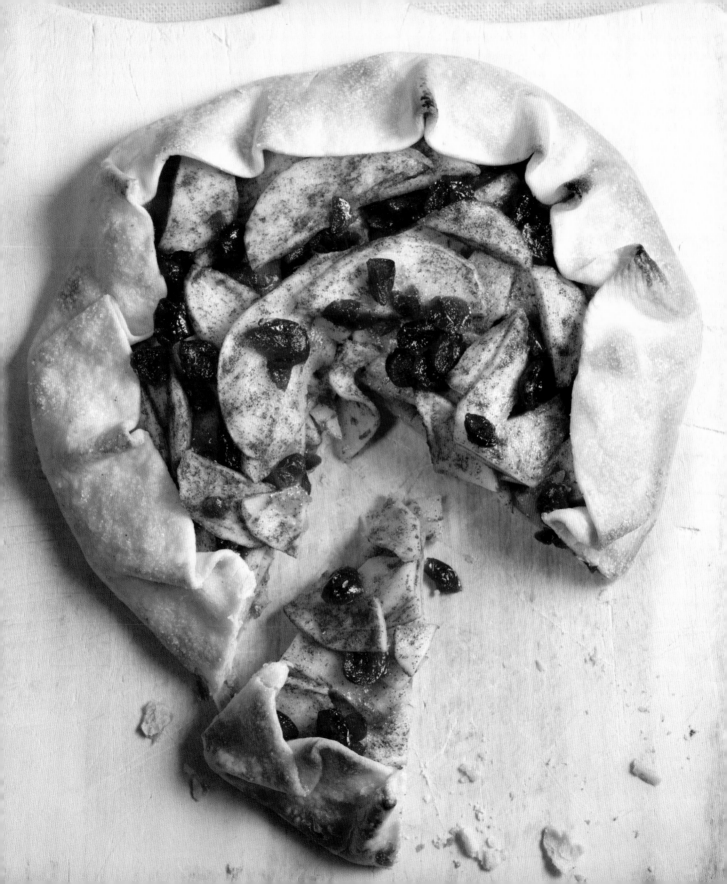

Lemon Tart

MAKES 8 TO 10 SERVINGS

1 **refrigerated pie crust (half of 15-ounce package)**

5 **eggs**

1 **tablespoon cornstarch**

1 **cup sugar**

½ **cup (1 stick) butter**

½ **cup lemon juice**

1. Position rack in center of oven. Preheat oven to 450°F.

2. Line 9-inch tart pan with pie crust, pressing to fit securely against side of pan. Trim off any excess crust. Prick bottom and side of crust with fork. Bake 9 to 10 minutes or until golden brown. Cool completely on wire rack. *Reduce oven temperature to 350°F.*

3. Meanwhile, whisk eggs and cornstarch in medium bowl until blended. Combine sugar, butter and lemon juice in small saucepan; cook and stir over medium-low heat just until butter melts. Whisk in egg mixture; cook 8 to 10 minutes or until thickened, stirring constantly. (Do not let mixture come to a boil.) Pour into medium bowl; stir 1 minute or until cooled slightly. Let cool 10 minutes. Pour cooled lemon curd into baked crust.

4. Bake 25 to 30 minutes or until set. Cool completely before cutting. Store leftovers in refrigerator.

Swedish Apple Pie

MAKES 8 SERVINGS

4 Granny Smith apples, peeled, cored and sliced

1 cup plus 1 tablespoon sugar, divided

1 tablespoon ground cinnamon

¾ cup (1½ sticks) butter, melted

1 cup all-purpose flour

½ cup chopped nuts

1 egg

1. Preheat oven to 350°F.

2. Spread apples in 9-inch deep-dish pie plate or 9-inch square baking dish. Combine 1 tablespoon sugar and cinnamon in small bowl; sprinkle over apples and drizzle with butter.

3. Combine remaining 1 cup sugar, flour, nuts and egg in medium bowl; mix well. (Mixture will be thick.) Spread batter over apples.

4. Bake 50 to 55 minutes or until top is golden brown.

Very Berry Tart

MAKES 8 SERVINGS

1 cup all-purpose flour

5 tablespoons Demerara cane sugar,* divided

5 tablespoons cold butter, cubed

¼ teaspoon salt

4 tablespoons ice water, divided

1 teaspoon almond extract

1 cup fresh or frozen sliced peeled peaches

1 cup fresh or frozen blackberries

½ cup fresh or frozen blueberries

1 tablespoon cornstarch

2 teaspoons orange peel

1 egg yolk

2 tablespoons slivered almonds

Or substitute turbinado sugar for the Demerara cane sugar.

1. Combine flour, 2 tablespoons sugar, butter and salt in food processor; process 1 minute or until crumbly. Slowly drizzle in 3 tablespoons ice water and almond extract; process 30 seconds to 1 minute or until mixture forms a ball. Wrap dough with plastic wrap; refrigerate 1 to 2 hours.

2. Preheat oven to 400°F. Line baking sheet with parchment paper. Roll out dough to ⅛-inch thickness on lightly floured surface; place on prepared baking sheet. Fold in edge of crust about 1 inch.

3. Combine peaches, blackberries, blueberries, remaining 3 tablespoons sugar, cornstarch and orange peel in medium bowl; mix well. Drain excess liquid. Mound fruit mixture in center of crust.

4. Whisk egg yolk and remaining 1 tablespoon ice water in small bowl; brush over dough. Sprinkle with almonds.

5. Bake 20 to 30 minutes or until crust is lightly browned. Remove to wire rack to cool slightly. Serve warm or at room temperature.

Lattice-Topped Cherry Pie

MAKES 8 SERVINGS

Pie Pastry (recipe follows)

6 **cups pitted sweet Bing cherries**

3/4 **cup plus 1 tablespoon sugar, divided**

3 **tablespoons plus 1 teaspoon cornstarch**

2 **tablespoons lemon juice**

1 **tablespoon half-and-half**

1. Prepare Pie Pastry. Preheat oven to 400°F.

2. Combine cherries, 3/4 cup sugar, cornstarch and lemon juice in large bowl; toss to coat. Let stand 15 minutes or until syrup forms.

3. Roll out one pastry disc into 12-inch circle (1/8 to 1/4 inch thick) on floured surface. Line 9-inch pie plate with pastry, letting excess drape over edge. Roll out remaining pastry disc into 11-inch circle; cut into 1/2-inch-wide strips.

4. Pour cherry filling into crust. Arrange pastry strips in lattice design over fruit. Tuck ends of strips under edge of bottom crust; seal edge. Brush pastry with half-and-half; sprinkle with remaining 1 tablespoon sugar. Cover loosely with foil.

5. Bake 30 minutes. Remove foil; bake 30 minutes or until filling is thick and bubbly and crust is golden brown. Cool on wire rack.

PIE PASTRY: Combine 2 1/4 cups all-purpose flour and 1/4 teaspoon salt in medium bowl. Cut in 1/2 cup cold cubed shortening and 2 tablespoons cold cubed butter with pastry blender or two knives until mixture resembles coarse crumbs. Gradually add 5 tablespoons cold water; mix with fork until dough forms, adding additional water as needed. Divide dough in half. Shape each half into a disc; wrap with plastic wrap. Refrigerate 30 minutes.

Chocolate Walnut Toffee Tart

MAKES 12 SERVINGS

2 cups all-purpose flour

1¼ cups plus 3 tablespoons sugar, divided

¾ cup (1½ sticks) butter, cut into pieces

2 egg yolks

1¼ cups whipping cream

1 teaspoon ground cinnamon

2 teaspoons vanilla

2 cups coarsely chopped walnuts

1¼ cups semisweet chocolate chips or chunks, divided

1. Preheat oven to 325°F. Line baking sheet with foil.

2. Combine flour and 3 tablespoons sugar in food processor; pulse just until blended. Scatter butter over flour mixture; process 20 seconds. Add egg yolks; process 10 seconds (mixture may be crumbly).

3. Press dough firmly and evenly into ungreased 10-inch tart pan with removable bottom or 9- or 10-inch pie plate. Bake 10 minutes or until surface is no longer shiny. Place tart pan on prepared baking sheet.

4. *Increase oven temperature to 375°F.* Combine remaining 1¼ cups sugar, cream and cinnamon in large saucepan; bring to a boil over medium-high heat. Reduce heat to medium-low; simmer 10 minutes, stirring frequently. Remove from heat; stir in vanilla.

5. Sprinkle walnuts and 1 cup chocolate chips evenly over crust. Pour cream mixture over top. Bake 35 to 40 minutes or until filling is bubbly and crust is lightly browned. Cool completely in pan on wire rack.

6. Place remaining ¼ cup chocolate chips in small resealable food storage bag. Microwave on HIGH 20 seconds; knead bag until chocolate is melted. Cut small hole in one corner of bag; drizzle chocolate over tart.

NOTE: Tart may be made up to 3 days in advance. Cover with plastic wrap and store at room temperature.

Classic Apple Pie

MAKES 8 SERVINGS

1 **package (15 ounces) refrigerated pie crusts (2 crusts)**

6 **cups sliced Granny Smith, Crispin or other firm-fleshed apples (about 6 medium)**

½ **cup sugar**

1 **tablespoon cornstarch**

2 **teaspoons lemon juice**

½ **teaspoon ground cinnamon**

½ **teaspoon vanilla**

⅛ **teaspoon salt**

⅛ **teaspoon ground nutmeg**

⅛ **teaspoon ground cloves**

1 **tablespoon whipping cream**

1. Let one crust stand at room temperature 15 minutes. Preheat oven to 350°F. Line 9-inch pie plate with crust.

2. Combine apples, sugar, cornstarch, lemon juice, cinnamon, vanilla, salt, nutmeg and cloves in large bowl; toss to coat. Pour into crust. Place second crust over apples; crimp edge to seal. Cut four slits in top crust; brush with cream.

3. Bake 40 minutes or until crust is golden brown. Cool completely on wire rack.

Strawberry Rhubarb Pie

MAKES 8 SERVINGS

Double-Crust Pie Pastry (recipe follows)

1½ **cups granulated sugar**

½ **cup cornstarch**

2 **tablespoons quick-cooking tapioca**

1 **tablespoon grated lemon peel**

¼ **teaspoon ground allspice**

4 **cups sliced rhubarb (1-inch pieces)**

3 **cups sliced fresh strawberries**

1 **egg, lightly beaten**

Coarse sugar (optional)

1. Prepare Double-Crust Pie Pastry. Preheat oven to 425°F.

2. Roll out one pastry disc into 11-inch circle on floured surface. Line 9-inch pie plate with pastry.

3. Combine granulated sugar, cornstarch, tapioca, lemon peel and allspice in large bowl. Add rhubarb and strawberries; toss to coat. Pour into crust.

4. Roll out remaining pastry disc into 10-inch circle; cut into ½-inch-wide strips. Arrange in lattice design over fruit. Seal and flute edge. Brush pastry with beaten egg; sprinkle with coarse sugar, if desired.

5. Bake 50 minutes or until filling is thick and bubbly and crust is golden brown. Cool on wire rack. Serve warm or at room temperature.

DOUBLE–CRUST PIE PASTRY: Combine 2½ cups all-purpose flour, 1 teaspoon salt and 1 teaspoon sugar in medium bowl. Cut in 1 cup (2 sticks) cubed unsalted butter with pastry blender or two knives until mixture resembles coarse crumbs. Drizzle ⅓ cup cold water over flour mixture, 2 tablespoons at a time, stirring just until dough comes together. Divide dough in half. Shape each half into a disc; wrap with plastic wrap. Refrigerate 30 minutes.

Praline Pumpkin Tart

MAKES 8 SERVINGS

1¼ cups all-purpose flour

1 tablespoon granulated sugar

¾ teaspoon salt, divided

¼ cup cold shortening, cut into small pieces

¼ cup (½ stick) cold butter, cut into small pieces

3 to 4 tablespoons cold water

1 can (15 ounces) solid-pack pumpkin

1 can (12 ounces) evaporated milk

⅔ cup packed brown sugar

2 eggs

1 teaspoon ground cinnamon

½ teaspoon ground ginger

¼ teaspoon ground cloves

Praline Topping (page 57)

1. Combine flour, granulated sugar and ¼ teaspoon salt in large bowl. Cut in shortening and butter with pastry blender or two knives until coarse crumbs form.

2. Sprinkle flour mixture with cold water, 1 tablespoon at a time. Toss with fork until mixture holds together. Shape into a ball; wrap with plastic wrap. Refrigerate about 1 hour or until chilled.

3. Roll out dough into 13×9-inch rectangle on lightly floured surface. Press into bottom and up sides of 11×7-inch baking dish. Cover with plastic wrap; refrigerate 30 minutes.

4. Preheat oven to 400°F. Pierce crust with tines of fork at ¼-inch intervals. Line baking dish with foil; fill with dried beans, uncooked rice or ceramic pie weights.

5. Bake 10 minutes or until set. Remove from oven; gently remove foil lining and beans. Bake 5 minutes or until crust is golden brown. Cool completely on wire rack.

6. Meanwhile, beat pumpkin, evaporated milk, brown sugar, eggs, cinnamon, remaining ½ teaspoon salt, ginger and cloves in large bowl with electric mixer at low speed until well blended. Pour into prepared crust. Bake 35 minutes.

7. Prepare Praline Topping. Sprinkle topping over tart. Bake 15 minutes or until knife inserted 1 inch from center comes out clean. Cool completely on wire rack.

PRALINE TOPPING: Combine ⅓ cup packed brown sugar, ⅓ cup chopped pecans and ⅓ cup quick oats in medium bowl. Cut in 1 tablespoon butter with pastry blender or two knives until coarse crumbs form.

Plum Walnut Pie
MAKES 8 SERVINGS

Single-Crust Pie Pastry
(recipe follows)

Oat Streusel (page 59)

8 **cups thinly sliced plums**

1/3 **cup granulated sugar**

1/3 **cup packed brown sugar**

3 **to 4 tablespoons all-purpose flour**

1 **tablespoon honey**

1/2 **teaspoon ground cinnamon**

1/4 **teaspoon ground ginger**

1/8 **teaspoon salt**

1/2 **cup candied walnuts***

*Candied walnuts are sold in packages in the baking section of the supermarket, or they may also be found in the produce section where salad ingredients are sold.

1. Prepare Single-Crust Pie Pastry and Oat Streusel.

2. Preheat oven to 425°F. Combine plums, granulated sugar, brown sugar, 3 tablespoons flour (use 4 tablespoons if plums are very juicy), honey, cinnamon, ginger and salt in large bowl; toss to coat.

3. Roll out pastry into 11-inch circle on floured surface. Line 9-inch pie plate with pastry; flute edge. Pour filling into crust; sprinkle with streusel. Place pie on baking sheet.

4. Bake 15 minutes. *Reduce oven temperature to 350°F.* Sprinkle pie with walnuts. Bake 30 minutes. Loosely tent pie with foil; bake 30 minutes or until filling is bubbly and crust is golden brown. Let stand at least 30 minutes before slicing.

SINGLE–CRUST PIE PASTRY: Combine 1 1/4 cups all-purpose flour and 1/2 teaspoon salt in medium bowl. Cut in 3 tablespoons cold cubed shortening and 3 tablespoons cold cubed butter with pastry blender or two knives until mixture resembles coarse crumbs. Combine 3 tablespoons ice water and 1/2 teaspoon cider vinegar in small bowl. Add to flour mixture; mix with fork until dough forms, adding additional water by teaspoonful as needed. Shape dough into a disc; wrap with plastic wrap. Refrigerate 30 minutes.

OAT STREUSEL: Combine ¼ cup all-purpose flour, ¼ cup old-fahioned oats, ¼ cup granulated sugar, ¼ cup packed light brown sugar and ⅛ teaspoon salt in medium bowl. Add ¼ cup (½ stick) cold cubed butter; mix with fingertips until mixture forms coarse crumbs.

Warm Apple Crostata

MAKES 4 TARTS (4 TO 8 SERVINGS)

1³/₄ cups all-purpose flour

¹/₃ cup granulated sugar

¹/₂ teaspoon plus ¹/₈ teaspoon salt, divided

³/₄ cup (1¹/₂ sticks) cold butter, cut into pieces

3 tablespoons ice water

2 teaspoons vanilla

8 Pink Lady or Honeycrisp apples (about 1¹/₂ pounds), peeled and cut into ¹/₄-inch slices

¹/₄ cup packed brown sugar

1 tablespoon lemon juice

1 teaspoon ground cinnamon

¹/₈ teaspoon ground nutmeg

4 teaspoons butter, cut into very small pieces

1 egg, beaten

1 to 2 teaspoons coarse sugar

Vanilla ice cream

Caramel sauce or ice cream topping

1. Combine flour, granulated sugar and ¹/₂ teaspoon salt in food processor; process 5 seconds. Add ³/₄ cup butter; process about 10 seconds or until mixture resembles coarse crumbs.

2. Combine ice water and vanilla in small bowl. With motor running, pour mixture through feed tube; process 12 seconds or until dough begins to come together. Shape dough into a disc; wrap with plastic wrap and refrigerate 30 minutes.

3. Meanwhile, combine apples, brown sugar, lemon juice, cinnamon, nutmeg and remaining ¹/₈ teaspoon salt in large bowl; toss to coat. Preheat oven to 400°F.

4. Line two baking sheets with parchment paper. Cut dough into four pieces; roll out each piece into 7-inch circle on floured surface. Place on prepared baking sheets; mound apples in center of dough circles (about 1 cup apples for each crostata). Fold or roll up edges of dough towards center to create rim of crostata. Dot apples with remaining 4 teaspoons butter. Brush dough with egg; sprinkle dough and apples with coarse sugar.

5. Bake about 20 minutes or until apples are tender and crust is golden brown. Serve warm with ice cream and caramel sauce.

Coconut Meringue Pie

MAKES 8 SERVINGS

1¼ cups sugar, divided

½ cup self-rising flour

1¼ cups milk

3 eggs, separated

2 tablespoons butter

1 teaspoon vanilla

1¼ cups flaked coconut, divided

1 baked (9-inch) pie crust

1. Preheat oven to 350°F.

2. Combine 1 cup sugar and flour in medium saucepan; mix well. Whisk in milk, egg yolks, butter and vanilla until well blended; cook over medium heat until mixture thickens, whisking constantly. Remove from heat; stir in 1 cup coconut. Pour into baked crust.

3. Beat egg whites in medium bowl with electric mixer at high speed until foamy. Gradually add remaining ¼ cup sugar, beating until soft peaks form. Spread meringue over filling; sprinkle with remaining ¼ cup coconut.

4. Bake 10 to 15 minutes or until meringue is golden brown. Cool completely on wire rack.

BREADS

Simple Golden Cornbread

MAKES 8 TO 10 SERVINGS

1¼ cups all-purpose flour

¾ cup yellow cornmeal

⅓ cup sugar

2 teaspoons baking powder

1 teaspoon salt

1¼ cups whole milk

¼ cup (½ stick) butter, melted

1 egg

Honey Butter (recipe follows, optional)

1. Preheat oven to 400°F. Spray 8-inch square baking dish or pan with nonstick cooking spray.

2. Combine flour, cornmeal, sugar, baking powder and salt in large bowl; mix well. Whisk milk, butter and egg in medium bowl until well blended. Add to flour mixture; stir just until dry ingredients are moistened. Pour batter into prepared baking dish.

3. Bake about 25 minutes or until golden brown and toothpick inserted into center comes out clean. Prepare Honey Butter, if desired. Serve with cornbread.

HONEY BUTTER: Beat 6 tablespoons (¾ stick) softened butter and ¼ cup honey in medium bowl with electric mixer at medium-high speed until light and creamy.

Cardamom Rolls

MAKES 12 ROLLS

DOUGH

- ½ **cup water**
- ½ **cup milk**
- 1 **tablespoon active dry yeast**
- ½ **cup plus 1 teaspoon granulated sugar, divided**
- ½ **cup (1 stick) butter, softened**
- 3 **eggs**
- ½ **teaspoon vanilla**
- 4 **cups all-purpose flour, divided**
- ¾ **teaspoon salt**

FILLING

- 2 **tablespoons butter, very soft**
- ¼ **cup packed brown sugar**
- 1½ **teaspoons ground cardamom**
- 1 **teaspoon ground cinnamon**
- 1 **tablespoon butter, melted**
  Pearl sugar (optional)

1. For dough, heat water and milk in small saucepan to about 115°F. Transfer to small bowl; stir in yeast and 1 teaspoon granulated sugar until dissolved. Let stand 5 minutes or until mixture is bubbly.

2. Beat butter and remaining ½ cup granulated sugar in large bowl with electric mixer at medium speed until light and fluffy. Add eggs, one at a time, beating well after each addition. Beat in vanilla. Reduce speed to low; beat in yeast mixture, 2 cups flour and salt. Beat at medium speed 2 minutes.

3. Replace paddle attachment with dough hook. Add remaining 2 cups flour; knead at low speed until most of flour is incorporated. Knead at medium speed 3 minutes (dough will be sticky). Cover and let rise in warm place about 1½ hours or until doubled in size. Stir down dough. Cover and refrigerate 2 hours or overnight.

4. Roll out dough into 18-inch square on floured surface. Spread 2 tablespoons butter over top half of dough; sprinkle with brown sugar, cardamom and cinnamon. Fold bottom of dough over filling; pinch ends to seal. Roll into 20×10-inch rectangle. Cut crosswise into 12 strips. Cut each strip lengthwise into two or three pieces, leaving them connected at the top. Holding uncut end, wrap cut dough around fingers; pull into knot shape, turning to expose some of filling. Place on baking sheet. Brush with melted butter; sprinkle with pearl sugar. Let stand 15 minutes.

5. Preheat oven to 375°F. Bake 15 to 20 minutes or until golden. Remove to wire rack to cool slightly. Serve warm.

Boston Black Coffee Bread

MAKES 8 SERVINGS

½ **cup rye flour**

½ **cup cornmeal**

½ **cup whole wheat flour**

1 **teaspoon baking soda**

½ **teaspoon salt**

¾ **cup strong brewed coffee, room temperature or cold**

⅓ **cup molasses**

¼ **cup canola oil**

¾ **cup raisins**

1. Preheat oven to 325°F. Grease and flour 9×5-inch loaf pan.

2. Combine rye flour, cornmeal, whole wheat flour, baking soda and salt in medium bowl; mix well. Stir in coffee, molasses and oil; stir until mixture forms thick batter. Fold in raisins. Pour batter into prepared pan.

3. Bake 50 minutes or until toothpick inserted into center comes out clean. Cool completely in pan on wire rack.

TIP: To cool hot coffee, pour it over 2 ice cubes in a measuring cup to measure ¾ cup total. Let stand 10 minutes to cool.

Focaccia

MAKES 12 SERVINGS

1 package (¼ ounce) active
   dry yeast

1 teaspoon sugar

1½ cups warm water (105° to
   110°F)

4 cups all-purpose flour, divided

7 tablespoons olive oil, divided

1 teaspoon salt

¼ cup bottled roasted red
   peppers, drained and cut
   into strips

¼ cup pitted black olives

1. Sprinkle yeast and sugar over warm water in large bowl; stir until dissolved. Let stand 5 minutes or until mixture is bubbly.

2. Add 3½ cups flour, 3 tablespoons oil and salt; stir until soft dough forms.

3. Turn out dough onto lightly floured surface. Knead 5 minutes or until smooth and elastic, gradually adding remaining flour to prevent sticking, if necessary. Shape dough into a ball. Place in large greased bowl; turn to grease top. Cover and let rise in warm place 1 hour or until doubled in size.

4. Brush 15×10-inch jelly-roll pan with 1 tablespoon oil. Punch down dough. Turn out dough onto lightly floured surface. Flatten into rectangle; roll out almost to size of pan. Transfer dough to pan; gently press to edges of pan. Poke surface of dough with end of wooden spoon handle, making indentations every 1 or 2 inches. Brush with remaining 3 tablespoons oil. Gently press peppers and olives into dough. Cover and let rise in warm place 30 minutes or until doubled in size. Preheat oven to 450°F.

5. Bake 12 to 18 minutes or until golden brown. Cut into squares or rectangles. Serve warm.

Treacle Bread (Brown Soda Bread)

MAKES 6 TO 8 SERVINGS

2 cups all-purpose flour, plus additional for dusting

1 cup whole wheat flour

1 teaspoon baking soda

1/2 teaspoon salt

1/2 teaspoon ground ginger

1 1/4 to 1 1/2 cups buttermilk

3 tablespoons dark molasses (preferably blackstrap)

1. Preheat oven to 375°F. Line baking sheet with parchment paper.

2. Combine 2 cups all-purpose flour, whole wheat flour, baking soda, salt and ginger in large bowl; mix well. Whisk 1 1/4 cups buttermilk and molasses in small bowl until blended.

3. Stir buttermilk mixture into flour mixture. Add additional buttermilk by tablespoonfuls if needed to make dry, rough dough. Turn out dough onto floured surface; knead 8 to 10 times or just until smooth. *Do not overknead.* Shape dough into round loaf about 1 1/2 inches thick. Place on prepared baking sheet.

4. Use floured knife to cut halfway through dough, scoring into quarters. Sprinkle top of dough with additional flour, if desired.

5. Bake about 35 minutes or until bread sounds hollow when tapped. Remove to wire rack to cool slightly. Serve warm.

Date-Nut Banana Braid

MAKES 1 LOAF

⅓ **cup milk**

2 **tablespoons butter**

3 **cups bread flour, divided**

¼ **cup plus 1 tablespoon sugar, divided**

1 **package (¼ ounce) rapid-rise yeast**

¾ **teaspoon salt**

½ **cup mashed ripe banana (about 1 large)**

1 **egg, beaten**

½ **cup chopped pitted dates**

½ **cup chopped walnuts**

1. Combine milk and butter in small saucepan; heat to 130°F. Combine 1 cup flour, ¼ cup sugar, yeast and salt in large bowl of electric stand mixer. Add milk mixture, banana and egg; beat at medium speed 3 minutes.

2. Replace paddle attachment with dough hook; beat in dates, walnuts and enough remaining flour to form soft dough. Knead at medium-low speed 6 to 8 minutes or until dough is smooth and elastic. Place dough in large greased bowl; turn to grease top. Cover and let rise in warm place about 30 minutes or until doubled in size.

3. Line baking sheet with parchment paper. Punch down dough. Divide dough into three pieces; roll each piece into 14-inch rope on lightly floured surface. Place ropes on prepared baking sheet; braid ropes and pinch ends to seal. Cover and let rise in warm place about 40 minutes or until doubled in size. Preheat oven to 375°F.

4. Sprinkle loaf with remaining 1 tablespoon sugar. Bake about 30 minutes or until golden brown and internal temperature reaches 200°F. Remove to wire rack to cool completely.

Cranberry Brie Bubble Bread

MAKES 12 SERVINGS

3 cups all-purpose flour

1 package (¼ ounce) rapid-rise yeast

1 teaspoon salt

1 cup warm water (120°F)

¼ cup plus 2 tablespoons butter, melted, divided

¾ cup finely chopped pecans or walnuts

¼ cup packed brown sugar

¼ teaspoon coarse salt

1 package (7 ounces) Brie cheese, cut into ¼-inch pieces

1 cup whole-berry cranberry sauce

1. Combine flour, yeast and 1 teaspoon salt in large bowl of electric stand mixer. Stir in warm water and 2 tablespoons butter to form rough dough. Knead with dough hook at low speed 5 to 7 minutes or until dough is smooth and elastic.

2. Shape dough into a ball. Place in greased bowl; turn to grease top. Cover and let rise in warm place about 45 minutes or until doubled in size.

3. Spray 2-quart baking dish or ovenproof bowl with nonstick cooking spray. Combine pecans, brown sugar and coarse salt in shallow bowl; mix well. Place remaining ¼ cup butter in another shallow bowl. Turn out dough onto lightly floured surface; pat and stretch into 9×6-inch rectangle. Cut dough into 1-inch pieces; roll into balls.

4. Dip balls of dough in butter; roll in pecan mixture to coat. Place in prepared baking dish, layering with Brie and spoonfuls of cranberry sauce. Cover and let rise in warm place about 45 minutes or until dough is puffy. Preheat oven to 350°F.

5. Bake 30 minutes or until dough is firm and filling is bubbly. Cool on wire rack 15 to 20 minutes. Serve warm.

Cheddar Biscuits

MAKES 15 BISCUITS

2 cups all-purpose flour

1 tablespoon sugar

1 tablespoon baking powder

2¼ teaspoons garlic powder, divided

¾ teaspoon plus pinch salt, divided

1 cup whole milk

½ cup (1 stick) plus 3 tablespoons butter, melted, divided

2 cups (8 ounces) shredded Cheddar cheese

½ teaspoon dried parsley flakes

1. Preheat oven to 450°F. Line baking sheet with parchment paper.

2. Combine flour, sugar, baking powder, 2 teaspoons garlic powder and ¾ teaspoon salt in large bowl; mix well. Add milk and ½ cup butter; stir just until dry ingredients are moistened. Stir in cheese just until blended. Drop scant ¼ cupfuls of dough about 1½ inches apart onto prepared baking sheet.

3. Bake 10 to 12 minutes or until golden brown.

4. Meanwhile, combine remaining 3 tablespoons butter, ¼ teaspoon garlic powder, pinch of salt and parsley flakes in small bowl; brush over biscuits immediately after removing from oven. Serve warm.

Three-Grain Bread

MAKES 1 LOAF

1 **cup whole wheat flour**

³/₄ **cup all-purpose flour**

1 **package (¹/₄ ounce) rapid-rise yeast**

1 **cup milk**

2 **tablespoons honey**

1 **tablespoon olive oil**

1 **teaspoon salt**

¹/₂ **cup plus 1 tablespoon old-fashioned oats, divided**

¹/₄ **cup whole grain cornmeal**

1 **egg beaten with 1 tablespoon water**

1. Combine whole wheat flour, all-purpose flour and yeast in large bowl of electric stand mixer. Combine milk, honey, oil and salt in small saucepan; heat over low heat until warm (110° to 120°F). Add to flour mixture; beat at high speed 3 minutes. Beat in ¹/₂ cup oats and cornmeal at low speed. If dough is too wet, add additional flour by teaspoonfuls until it begins to come together.

2. Replace paddle attachment with dough hook. Knead at medium speed 5 minutes or until dough forms a ball. Place dough in large greased bowl; turn to grease top. Cover and let rise in warm place about 1 hour or until dough is puffy and does not spring back when touched.

3. Punch dough down; shape into 8-inch-long loaf. Place on baking sheet lightly sprinkled with cornmeal. Cover and let rise in warm place about 45 minutes or until almost doubled in size. Preheat oven to 375°F.

4. Make shallow slash down center of loaf with sharp knife. Brush lightly with egg mixture; sprinkle with remaining 1 tablespoon oats.

5. Bake 30 minutes or until loaf sounds hollow when tapped (internal temperature of 200°F). Cool on wire rack.

Pumpkin Cinnamon Rolls

MAKES 12 ROLLS

DOUGH

- 1/2 **cup milk**
- 1/4 **cup (1/2 stick) butter**
- 1 **package (1/4 ounce) rapid-rise yeast**
- 2/3 **cup canned pumpkin**
- 1/2 **cup packed brown sugar**
- 1 **egg**
- 1 **teaspoon salt**
- 1/2 **teaspoon pumpkin pie spice**
- 31/2 **to 4 cups all-purpose flour**

FILLING

- 3/4 **cup packed brown sugar**
- 2 **teaspoons ground cinnamon**
  Pinch salt
- 1/4 **cup (1/2 stick) butter, softened**

GLAZE

- 2 **cups powdered sugar**
- 4 **ounces cream cheese, softened**
- 1 **to 2 tablespoons milk**
- 1/2 **teaspoon vanilla**

1. For dough, heat milk and 1/4 cup butter to 120°F in small microwavable bowl. Stir in yeast; let stand 5 minutes or until mixture is bubbly.

2. Combine pumpkin, 1/2 cup brown sugar, egg, 1 teaspoon salt, pumpkin pie spice and milk mixture in large bowl of electric stand mixer; beat at low speed until well blended. Add 31/2 cups flour; knead with dough hook at low speed 5 to 7 minutes or until dough is smooth and elastic, adding additional flour by tablespoonfuls if necessary.

3. Shape dough into a ball. Place in large greased bowl; turn to grease top. Cover and let rise in warm place 1 hour and 15 minutes or until doubled in size.

4. Spray 13×9-inch baking pan with nonstick cooking spray. Combine 3/4 cup brown sugar, cinnamon and pinch of salt in small bowl; mix well. Punch down dough; roll out into 18×14-inch rectangle on lightly floured surface. Spread 1/4 cup softened butter over dough; sprinkle with brown sugar mixture. Starting with long end, roll up dough tightly jelly-roll style; pinch seam to seal. Trim ends; cut roll crosswise into 12 slices. Place slices cut sides up in prepared pan. Cover and let rise in warm place 45 minutes or until almost doubled. Preheat oven to 350°F.

5. Bake about 20 minutes or until lightly browned. Meanwhile, for glaze, whisk powdered sugar, cream cheese, 1 tablespoon milk and vanilla in medium bowl until smooth. Add remaining 1 tablespoon milk to thin glaze, if desired. Drizzle over warm rolls.

Garlic Knots
MAKES 20 KNOTS

¾ **cup warm water (105° to 115°F)**

1 **package (¼ ounce) active dry yeast**

1 **teaspoon sugar**

2¼ **cups all-purpose flour, plus additional for work surface**

2 **tablespoons olive oil, divided**

1½ **teaspoons salt, divided**

4 **tablespoons (½ stick) butter, divided**

1 **tablespoon minced garlic**

¼ **teaspoon garlic powder**

½ **cup grated Parmesan cheese**

2 **tablespoons chopped fresh parsley**

½ **teaspoon dried oregano**

1. Combine warm water, yeast and sugar in large bowl of electric stand mixer; stir to dissolve yeast. Let stand 5 minutes or until mixture is bubbly. Stir in 2¼ cups flour, 1 tablespoon oil and 1 teaspoon salt; knead with dough hook at low speed 5 minutes or until dough is smooth and elastic. Shape dough into a ball. Place in large greased bowl; turn to grease top. Cover and let rise 1 hour or until doubled in size.

2. Melt 2 tablespoons butter in small saucepan over low heat. Add remaining 1 tablespoon oil, ½ teaspoon salt, minced garlic and garlic powder; cook over very low heat 5 minutes. Pour into small bowl; set aside.

3. Preheat oven to 400°F. Line baking sheet with parchment paper.

4. Turn out dough onto lightly floured surface. Punch down dough; let stand 10 minutes. Roll out dough into 10×8-inch rectangle. Cut into 20 (2-inch) squares. Roll each piece into 8-inch rope; tie in a knot. Place knots on prepared baking sheet; brush with garlic mixture.

5. Bake 10 minutes or until knots are lightly browned. Meanwhile, melt remaining 2 tablespoons butter. Combine cheese, parsley and oregano in small bowl; mix well. Brush melted butter over baked knots immediatly after baking; sprinkle with cheese mixture. Cool slightly; serve warm.

breads | # Peanut Butter Bran Muffins
MAKES 12 MUFFINS

½ **cup peanut butter**

2 **tablespoons butter, softened**

¼ **cup packed brown sugar**

1 **egg**

1 **cup whole bran cereal**

1 **cup milk**

¾ **cup all-purpose flour**

1 **tablespoon baking powder**

½ **teaspoon salt**

½ **cup dark raisins**

1. Heat oven to 400°F. Spray 12 standard (2½-inch) muffin cups with nonstick cooking spray or line with paper baking cups.

2. Combine peanut butter, butter, brown sugar and egg in food pocessor; process 5 to 10 seconds or until smooth. Add cereal and milk; pulse just until blended.

3. Add flour, baking powder and salt; pulse 2 to 3 times or just until flour is moistened. (Do not overprocess. Batter should be lumpy.) Sprinkle raisins over batter; pulse just until raisins are incorporated. Spoon batter into prepared muffin cups, filling about three-fourths full.

4. Bake 20 to 25 minutes or until golden brown. Cool in pan 5 minutes; remove to wire rack. Serve warm.

Beer Pretzels

MAKES 12 PRETZELS

¼ cup warm water

1 package (¼ ounce) active dry yeast

1 tablespoon sugar

1 tablespoon olive oil

1 teaspoon kosher salt, divided

1 cup brown ale, at room temperature

3¾ to 4 cups all-purpose flour

2 cups hot water

1 teaspoon baking soda

1 egg, well beaten

2 tablespoons butter, melted

Mustard (optional)

1. Place warm water in large bowl; sprinkle with yeast. Let stand 5 minutes or until mixture is bubbly. Add sugar, oil, ¾ teaspoon salt, ale and 3¾ cups flour; stir to form soft dough. Knead on floured surface 6 to 8 minutes or until smooth and elastic, adding additional flour by tablespoonfuls if necessary.

2. Place dough in large bowl; turn to grease top. Cover and let stand in warm place 45 minutes or until doubled in size. Punch down dough. Divide into 12 pieces.

3. Roll each piece into a rope about 20 inches long. If dough becomes too difficult to roll, let stand 10 minutes. Shape ropes into pretzels.

4. Preheat oven to 425°F. Line baking sheet with parchment paper or spray with nonstick cooking spray. Stir hot water into baking soda in pie plate until well blended. Dip pretzels into mixture; place on baking sheet. Cover loosely and let stand in warm place 15 to 20 minutes. Brush pretzels with egg; sprinkle with remaining ¼ teaspoon salt.

5. Bake 10 minutes or until golden brown. Brush pretzels with butter. Serve with mustard, if desired.

Cherry, Almond and Chocolate Twist

MAKES 8 TO 10 SERVINGS

1 cup cold water

1 cup dried sweet or sour cherries

1/2 cup granulated sugar, divided

1 package (1/4 ounce) active dry yeast

1/4 cup warm water (105° to 115°F)

1/2 cup plus 1 tablespoon milk, divided

3 tablespoons butter, cut into pieces

2 eggs, divided

1 tablespoon grated lemon peel

1/2 teaspoon salt

1/2 teaspoon almond extract

2 1/2 to 2 3/4 cups all-purpose flour

1/2 cup canned almond filling (about 12 ounces)

3/4 cup semisweet chocolate chips

Almond Glaze (page 91)

1. Combine cold water, cherries and 1/4 cup granulated sugar in small saucepan; bring to a boil over high heat, stirring frequently. Remove from heat; cover and set aside.

2. Dissolve yeast in 1/4 cup warm water in large bowl of electric stand mixer; let stand 5 minutes or until bubbly.

3. Meanwhile, heat 1/2 cup milk and butter in medium saucepan over high heat until milk bubbles around edge of saucepan, stirring constantly (butter does not need to melt completely). Remove from heat; stir occasionally until milk is warm to the touch.

4. Add milk mixture to yeast mixture. Stir in remaining 1/4 cup granulated sugar, 1 egg, lemon peel, salt and almond extract until well blended. Add 2 1/4 cups flour; beat at low speed until dough forms a sticky ball. Stir in enough remaining flour to make a soft dough.

5. Replace paddle attachment with dough hook. Knead at low speed about 5 minutes or until dough is smooth and elastic, adding additional flour if necessary to prevent sticking. Shape dough into a ball. Place in large greased bowl; turn to grease top. Cover and let rise in warm place 1 to 2 hours or until doubled in size.

6. Preheat oven to 350°F. Line baking sheet with parchment paper. Punch down dough several times. Turn out dough onto lightly floured surface; knead 10 to 12 times or until dough is smooth. Shape dough into 10-inch

log; flatten slightly. Roll out dough into 18×8-inch rectangle with lightly floured rolling pin.

7. Drain cherries. Spread almond filling over dough; sprinkle with cherries and chocolate chips. Starting with long side, roll up dough jelly-roll style; pinch seam to seal.

8. Transfer roll to prepared baking sheet. Use long sharp knife to cut roll in half lengthwise (through all layers). Turn halves cut sides up on baking sheet; carefully twist halves together, keeping cut sides facing up as much as possible. Press ends together to seal and tuck underneath. Whisk remaining egg and 1 tablespoon milk in small bowl; brush lightly over dough.

9. Bake 30 minutes or until golden brown. (Cover loosely with foil if browning too quickly.) Cool on baking sheet 5 minutes; remove to wire rack to cool completely.

10. Prepare Almond Glaze; drizzle over coffeecake. Let stand until set.

ALMOND GLAZE: Stir ½ cup powdered sugar, 2 teaspoons milk and ¼ teaspoon almond extract in small bowl until smooth. Add additional milk if necessary to reach desired consistency.

Oat and Whole Wheat Scones

MAKES 8 SCONES

1 cup old-fashioned oats

1 cup whole wheat flour

½ cup all-purpose flour

¼ cup sugar

1 tablespoon baking powder

¼ teaspoon salt

½ cup (1 stick) butter, cut into small pieces

½ cup whipping cream

1 egg

¾ cup dried cherries

1. Preheat oven to 425°F. Line baking sheet with parchment paper.

2. Combine oats, whole wheat flour, all-purpose flour, sugar, baking powder and salt in large bowl. Cut in butter with pastry blender or two forks until mixture resembles coarse crumbs. Whisk cream and egg in small bowl. Stir into flour mixture until dough comes together. Stir in cherries.

3. Turn out dough onto lightly floured surface. Shape dough into 8-inch disc about ¾ inch thick. Cut into eight wedges; place 1 inch apart on prepared baking sheet.

4. Bake 18 to 20 minutes. Serve warm.

Bacon Cheddar Monkey Bread

MAKES 12 SERVINGS

1³/₄ cups (7 ounces) shredded sharp Cheddar cheese

12 ounces bacon, crisp-cooked and chopped (about 1 cup)

¹/₄ cup finely chopped green onions

2³/₄ to 3 cups all-purpose flour, divided

1 package (¹/₄ ounce) rapid-rise yeast

1 teaspoon salt

1 cup warm water (120°F)

2 tablespoons olive oil

¹/₃ cup butter, melted

1 egg

1. Combine cheese, bacon and green onions in medium bowl; mix well.

2. Combine 1¹/₂ cups flour, yeast and salt in large bowl of electric stand mixer; stir to combine. Add warm water and oil; beat at medium speed 3 minutes.

3. Replace paddle attachment with dough hook. Add 1¹/₄ cups flour; knead at medium speed until dough comes together. Add 1 cup cheese mixture; knead at medium-low speed 6 to 8 minutes or until dough is smooth and elastic, adding remaining ¹/₄ cup flour if necessary to clean side of bowl. Place dough in large greased bowl; turn to grease top. Cover and let rise in warm place about 30 minutes or until doubled in size.

4. Generously spray 12-cup (10-inch) bundt pan with nonstick cooking spray. Whisk butter and egg in shallow bowl until blended. Punch down dough. Roll 1-inch pieces of dough into balls. Dip balls in butter mixture; roll in remaining cheese mixture to coat. Layer balls in prepared pan. Cover and let rise in warm place about 40 minutes or until almost doubled in size. Preheat oven to 375°F.

5. Bake about 35 minutes or until golden brown. Loosen edges of bread with knife; invert onto wire rack. Cool 5 minutes; serve warm.

COOKIES

Lemony Butter Cookies

MAKES ABOUT 2½ DOZEN COOKIES

½ **cup (1 stick) butter, softened**

½ **cup granulated sugar**

1 **egg**

1½ **cups all-purpose flour**

2 **tablespoons fresh lemon juice**

1 **teaspoon grated lemon peel**

½ **teaspoon baking powder**

⅛ **teaspoon salt**

Sparkling sugar (optional)

1. Beat butter and granulated sugar in large bowl with electric mixer at medium speed until creamy. Beat in egg until light and fluffy. Beat in flour, lemon juice, lemon peel, baking powder and salt at low speed just until blended. Wrap dough with plastic wrap; refrigerate about 2 hours or until firm.

2. Preheat oven to 350°F.

3. Roll out dough, a small portion at a time, to ¼-inch thickness on well-floured surface. (Keep remaining dough in refrigerator.) Cut out dough with 3-inch fluted or round cookie cutter. Transfer cutouts to ungreased cookie sheets. Sprinkle with sparkling sugar, if desired.

4. Bake 8 to 10 minutes or until edges are lightly browned. Cool on cookie sheets 1 minute; remove to wire racks to cool completely.

Marshmallow Sandwich Cookies

MAKES ABOUT 2 DOZEN SANDWICH COOKIES

2 cups all-purpose flour

$1/2$ cup unsweetened cocoa powder

2 teaspoons baking soda

$1/2$ teaspoon salt

$1^1/2$ cups sugar, divided

$2/3$ cup butter, softened

$1/4$ cup light corn syrup

1 egg

1 teaspoon vanilla

24 large marshmallows

1. Preheat oven to 350°F. Combine flour, cocoa, baking soda and salt in medium bowl; mix well.

2. Beat $1^1/4$ cups sugar and butter in large bowl with electric mixer at medium-high speed until light and fluffy. Beat in corn syrup, egg and vanilla until blended. Add flour mixture; beat at low speed until blended. Cover and refrigerate 15 minutes or until dough is firm enough to shape into balls.

3. Place remaining $1/4$ cup sugar in small bowl. Shape dough into 1-inch balls; roll in sugar to coat. Place 3 inches apart on ungreased cookie sheets.

4. Bake 10 to 11 minutes or until set. Cool on cookie sheets 3 minutes; remove to wire racks to cool completely.

5. Place one cookie on microwavable plate. Top with one marshmallow. Microwave on HIGH about 10 seconds or until marshmallow is softened. Immediately place another cookie, flat side down, on top of hot marshmallow; press together. Repeat with remaining cookies and marshmallows.

Snickerdoodles

MAKES ABOUT 3 DOZEN COOKIES

3/4 cup plus 2 tablespoons sugar, **divided**

2 teaspoons ground cinnamon, **divided**

1 1/3 cups all-purpose flour

1 teaspoon cream of tartar

1/2 teaspoon baking soda

1/2 teaspoon salt

1/2 cup (1 stick) butter, softened

1 egg

1. Preheat oven to 375°F. Line cookie sheets with parchment paper. Combine 2 tablespoons sugar and 1 teaspoon cinnamon in small bowl; mix well.

2. Combine flour, remaining 1 teaspoon cinnamon, cream of tartar, baking soda and salt in medium bowl; mix well.

3. Beat remaining 3/4 cup sugar and butter in large bowl with electric mixer at medium speed until creamy. Beat in egg until blended. Gradually add flour mixture, beating at low speed until stiff dough forms.

4. Roll dough into 1-inch balls; roll in cinnamon-sugar mixture to coat. Place on prepared cookie sheets.

5. Bake 10 minutes or until set. *Do not overbake*. Remove to wire racks to cool completely.

Chocolate Hazelnut Sandwich Cookies

MAKES 2½ DOZEN SANDWICH COOKIES

¾ **cup (1½ sticks) butter, slightly softened**

¾ **cup sugar**

3 **egg yolks**

1 **teaspoon vanilla**

2 **cups all-purpose flour**

¼ **teaspoon salt**

⅔ **cup chocolate hazelnut spread**

1. Beat butter and sugar in large bowl with electric mixer at medium speed 1 minute. Beat in egg yolks and vanilla until well blended. Add flour and salt; beat just until combined. Divide dough in half. Shape each piece into 6×1½-inch log. Wrap with plastic wrap; refrigerate at least 2 hours or until firm.

2. Preheat oven to 350°F. Line cookie sheets with parchment paper.

3. Cut dough into ⅛-inch-thick slices; place 1 inch apart on prepared cookie sheets.

4. Bake 10 to 12 minutes or until edges are lightly browned. Cool on cookie sheets 5 minutes; remove to wire racks to cool completely.

5. Spread 1 teaspoon hazelnut spread on flat side of half of cookies; top with remaining cookies. Store covered in airtight container.

NOTE: Dough can be refrigerated up to 3 days or frozen for up to 1 month.

Refrigerator Cookies
MAKES ABOUT 4 DOZEN COOKIES

½ cup sugar

¼ cup light corn syrup

¼ cup (½ stick) butter, softened

1 egg

1 teaspoon vanilla

1¾ cups all-purpose flour

¼ teaspoon baking soda

¼ teaspoon salt

Colored nonpareils, decors and/or decorating sugars (optional)

1. Beat sugar, corn syrup and butter in large bowl until well blended. Add egg and vanilla; mix well.

2. Combine flour, baking soda and salt in medium bowl. Add to sugar mixture; stir until blended. Shape dough into two rolls 1½ inches in diameter. Wrap with plastic wrap. Freeze 1 hour.

3. Preheat oven to 350°F. Line baking sheets with parchment paper. Cut dough into ¼-inch-thick slices; place 1 inch apart on prepared cookie sheets. Sprinkle with nonpareils, if desired.

4. Bake 8 to 10 minutes or until edges are golden brown. Remove to wire racks to cool completely.

VARIATIONS: Add 2 tablespoons unsweetened cocoa powder to dough for chocolate cookies. For sugar-rimmed cookies, roll logs in colored sugar before slicing.

Peanutty Double Chip Cookies

MAKES ABOUT 3 DOZEN COOKIES

½ cup (1 stick) butter, softened

¾ cup granulated sugar

¾ cup packed brown sugar

2 eggs

1 teaspoon baking soda

1 teaspoon vanilla

2 cups all-purpose flour

1 cup chunky peanut butter

1 cup semisweet or milk chocolate chips

1 cup peanut butter chips

1. Preheat oven to 350°F. Line cookie sheets with parchment paper or spray with nonstick cooking spray.

2. Beat butter, granulated sugar and brown sugar in large bowl with electric mixer at medium speed until well blended. Add eggs, baking soda and vanilla; beat until light. Add flour and peanut butter; beat at low speed until dough is stiff and smooth. Stir in chocolate and peanut butter chips.

3. Drop dough by heaping tablespoonfuls 2 inches apart onto prepared cookie sheets. Press cookies down with tines of fork to flatten slightly.

4. Bake 12 minutes or until set but not browned. *Do not overbake.* Remove to wire racks to cool completely.

Black and White Cookies

MAKES 1½ DOZEN COOKIES

COOKIES

- 2 **cups all-purpose flour**
- 1 **tablespoon cornstarch**
- ¾ **teaspoon baking soda**
- ½ **teaspoon salt**
- ¾ **cup (1½ sticks) butter, softened**
- 1 **cup granulated sugar**
- 2 **eggs**
- 1 **teaspoon vanilla**
- ½ **teaspoon grated lemon peel**
- ⅔ **cup buttermilk**

ICINGS

- 3½ **cups powdered sugar, divided**
- 3 **tablespoons plus 3 teaspoons boiling water, divided**
- 1 **tablespoon lemon juice**
- 2 **teaspoons corn syrup, divided**
- ¼ **teaspoon vanilla**
- 3 **ounces unsweetened chocolate, melted**

1. Preheat oven to 350°F. Line cookie sheets with parchment paper.

2. For cookies, combine flour, cornstarch, baking soda and salt in small bowl; mix well.

3. Beat butter and granulated sugar in large bowl with electric mixer at medium-high speed until light and fluffy. Beat in eggs, one at a time until well blended. Beat in 1 teaspoon vanilla and lemon peel. Add flour mixture alternately with buttermilk, beating at low speed until blended after each addition. Scrape bowl with rubber spatula and stir several times to bring dough together. Using dampened hands, shape 3 tablespoons dough into a ball for each cookie. Place 3 inches apart on prepared cookie sheets.

4. Bake 13 to 15 minutes or until tops are puffed and edges are lightly browned. Cool on cookie sheets 1 minute. Remove to wire racks; trim any crispy browned edges, if desired. Cool completely.

5. For icings, place 2 cups powdered sugar in small bowl; whisk in 1 tablespoon boiling water, lemon juice and 1 teaspoon corn syrup until smooth and well blended. If necessary, add additional 1 teaspoon boiling water to make smooth, thick and spreadable glaze. Spread icing over half of each cookie; place on wire rack or waxed paper to set.

6. Place remaining 1½ cups powdered sugar in another small bowl; whisk in 2 tablespoons boiling water, remaining 1 teaspoon corn syrup and ¼ teaspoon vanilla. Whisk in chocolate until smooth and well blended.

If necessary, add additional 1 to 2 teaspoons boiling water to make smooth, thick and spreadable glaze. Spread icing on other side of each cookie. Place on wire rack; let stand until set. Cookies are best the day they are made, but they can be stored in airtight container at room temperature 1 to 2 days.

Gingery Oat and Molasses Cookies

MAKES ABOUT 4 DOZEN COOKIES

1 cup all-purpose flour

¾ cup whole wheat flour

½ cup old-fashioned oats

1½ teaspoons baking powder

1½ teaspoons ground ginger

1 teaspoon baking soda

½ teaspoon ground cinnamon

¼ teaspoon salt

¾ cup sugar

½ cup (1 stick) butter, softened

1 egg

¼ cup molasses

¼ teaspoon vanilla

1 cup chopped crystallized ginger

½ cup chopped walnuts

1. Combine all-purpose flour, whole wheat flour, oats, baking powder, ground ginger, baking soda, cinnamon and salt in medium bowl; mix well. Beat sugar and butter in large bowl with electric mixer at high speed until light and fluffy. Beat in egg, molasses and vanilla. Gradually beat in flour mixture just until blended. Stir in crystallized ginger and walnuts.

2. Shape dough into two 8- to 10-inch logs. Wrap with plastic wrap; refrigerate 1 to 3 hours.

3. Preheat oven to 350°F. Line cookie sheets with parchment paper or spray with nonstick cooking spray.

4. Cut logs into ⅓-inch slices; place 1½ inches apart on prepared cookie sheets.

5. Bake 12 to 14 minutes or until set. Cool on cookie sheets 5 minutes; remove to wire racks to cool completely.

Chocolate Chip Sandwich Cookies

MAKES 16 SANDWICH COOKIES

- ¾ cup plus ⅓ cup packed brown sugar
- ½ cup (1 stick) butter, softened
- 1 egg
- 1 teaspoon vanilla
- ¾ teaspoon baking soda
- ½ teaspoon salt
- 1¾ cups all-purpose flour
- 3 cups semisweet chocolate chips, divided
- 6 tablespoons whipping cream

1. Preheat oven to 350°F. Line cookie sheets with parchment paper.

2. Beat brown sugar and butter in large bowl with electric mixer at medium speed 5 minutes or until light and fluffy. Add egg and vanilla; beat until well blended. Beat in baking soda and salt. Slowly add flour, beating at low speed until blended. Stir in 1½ cups chocolate chips. Drop heaping tablespoonfuls of dough 2 inches apart onto prepared cookie sheets.

3. Bake about 10 minutes or until cookies are just beginning to brown around edges but are still very soft in center. (Cookies will look underbaked.) Cool on cookie sheets 5 minutes; remove to wire racks to cool completely.

4. While cookies are baking, prepare ganache filling. Heat cream to a simmer in microwave oven or on stovetop. Add remaining 1½ cups chocolate chips to cream; let stand 1 minute. Stir until smooth. Refrigerate 1 hour, stirring occasionally. (Filling should be thick enough to spread and still be shiny when stirred.)

5. Spread heaping tablespoonful ganache filling onto bottoms of half of cookies. Top with remaining cookies.

PB and J Thumbprint Cookies

MAKES ABOUT 3½ DOZEN COOKIES

2 cups old-fashioned oats

1⅓ cups plus 1 tablespoon all-purpose flour

¾ teaspoon baking soda

½ teaspoon baking powder

½ teaspoon salt

¼ teaspoon ground cinnamon

1 cup packed brown sugar

¾ cup (1½ sticks) butter, softened

¼ cup granulated sugar

¼ cup chunky peanut butter

1 egg

1 tablespoon honey

1 teaspoon vanilla

½ cup chopped peanuts (unsalted or honey-roasted)

½ cup grape jelly or favorite flavor jam

1. Preheat oven to 350°F. Line cookie sheets with parchment paper.

2. Combine oats, flour, baking soda, baking powder, salt and cinnamon in medium bowl; mix well. Beat brown sugar, butter and granulated sugar in large bowl with electric mixer at medium speed until light and fluffy. Add peanut butter, egg, honey and vanilla; beat until well blended. Gradually add flour mixture, about ½ cup at a time; beat just until blended. Stir in peanuts. Drop dough by rounded tablespoonfuls onto prepared cookie sheets.

3. Bake 10 minutes. Press center of each cookie with back of teaspoon to make slight indentation; fill with about ½ teaspoon jelly. Bake 4 to 6 minutes or until puffed and golden. Cool on cookie sheets 5 minutes; remove to wire racks to cool completely.

Chocolate Cookie Pops

MAKES 16 COOKIES

2 cups all-purpose flour

1/2 cup unsweetened cocoa powder

1/2 teaspoon baking powder

1/2 teaspoon salt

1 cup (2 sticks) butter, softened

1 cup granulated sugar, plus additional for flattening cookies

1/2 cup packed brown sugar

1 egg

1 teaspoon vanilla

1 cup white chocolate chips or semisweet chocolate chips

1 teaspoon shortening

Sprinkles or decors

1. Preheat oven to 350°F. Combine flour, cocoa, baking powder and salt in small bowl; mix well. Beat butter, 1 cup granulated sugar and brown sugar in large bowl with electric mixer at medium speed until light and fluffy. Beat in egg and vanilla until well blended. Gradually beat in flour mixture at low speed.

2. Drop dough by scant 1/4 cupfuls (2 ounces each) 3 inches apart onto ungreased cookie sheets. Dip bottom of glass in granulated sugar; press dough to flatten cookies to 2 inches in diameter. Insert popsicle stick 1 1/2 inches into each cookie.

3. Bake 14 to 16 minutes or until cookies are set. If necessary, trim uneven crispy edges from cookies with sharp knife. Cool on cookie sheets 5 minutes; remove to wire racks to cool completely.

4. Combine white chocolate chips and shortening in small resealable food storage bag; seal bag. Microwave on HIGH 30 seconds. Turn bag; microwave 30 seconds to 1 minute or until chips are melted. Knead bag until chocolate is smooth.

5. Cut off small corner of bag; pipe melted chocolate over cookies. Decorate with sprinkles. Let stand 30 minutes or until chocolate is set.

TIP: Try using colorful paper straws instead of wooden pop sticks. Bake cookies as directed without sticks and immediately remove to wire racks. Carefully insert a straw into each hot cookie all the way to the top. Cool completely.

Raspberry Macarons

MAKES 16 TO 20 MACARON SANDWICH COOKIES

1½ **cups powdered sugar**

1 **cup blanched almond flour***

3 **egg whites, at room temperature****

1 **tablespoon raspberry liqueur**

Red paste food coloring

¼ **cup granulated sugar**

Raspberry jam***

*Almond flour, also called almond powder, is available in the specialty flour section of the supermarket.

**For best results, separate the eggs while cold. Leave the egg whites at room temperature for 3 or 4 hours. Reserve yolks in refrigerator for another use.

***Cookies may also be filled with chocolate ganache; see recipe on page 112, step 4.

1. Line two cookie sheets with parchment paper. Double cookie sheets by placing another sheet underneath each to protect macarons from burning or cracking. (Do not use insulated cookie sheets.)

2. Combine powdered sugar and almond flour in food processor. Pulse 2 to 3 minutes or until well combined into very fine powder, scraping bowl occasionally. Sift mixture twice. Discard any remaining large pieces.

3. Beat egg whites in large bowl with electric mixer at high speed until foamy. Add liqueur and food coloring. Gradually add granulated sugar, beating at high speed 2 to 3 minutes or until mixture forms stiff, shiny peaks, scraping bowl occasionally.

4. Add half of sifted flour mixture to egg whites. Stir with spatula to combine (about 12 strokes). Repeat with remaining flour mixture. Mix about 15 strokes more by pressing against side of bowl and scooping from bottom until batter is smooth and shiny. Check consistency by dropping spoonful of batter onto plate. It should have a peak which quickly relaxes back into batter. *Do not overmix or undermix.*

5. Attach ½-inch plain piping tip to pastry bag. Scoop batter into bag. Pipe 1-inch circles onto prepared cookie sheet about 2 inches apart. Rap cookie sheet on flat surface to remove air bubbles and set aside. Repeat with remaining batter. Let macarons rest, uncovered, until tops harden slightly; this takes from 15 minutes on dry days to 1 hour in more humid conditions. Gently touch top of macaron to check. When batter does not stick, macarons are ready to bake.

6. Meanwhile, preheat oven to 375°F. Place rack in center of oven. Place one sheet of macarons in oven. *After 5 minutes, reduce oven temperature to 325°F.* Bake 10 to 13 minutes, checking at 5 minute intervals. If macarons begin to brown, cover loosely with foil and reduce oven temperature or prop oven open slightly with wooden spoon. Repeat with remaining cookie sheet. Cool completely on sheets on wire rack.

7. While cooling, if cookies appear to be sticking to parchment, lift parchment edges and spray underneath lightly with water. Steam will help release macarons.

8. Match same size cookies; spread bottom macaron with raspberry jam and top with another. Store macarons in covered container in refrigerator 4 to 5 days or freeze for longer storage.

Chocolate-Dipped Cinnamon Thins

MAKES ABOUT 2 DOZEN COOKIES

1¼ **cups all-purpose flour**

1½ **teaspoons ground cinnamon**

¼ **teaspoon salt**

1 **cup (2 sticks) butter, softened**

1 **cup powdered sugar**

1 **egg**

1 **teaspoon vanilla**

4 **ounces chopped bittersweet chocolate bar, melted**

1. Combine flour, cinnamon and salt in small bowl; mix well. Beat butter in large bowl with electric mixer at medium speed until creamy. Add powdered sugar; beat until well blended. Beat in egg and vanilla. Gradually add flour mixture at low speed, beating just until blended.

2. Place dough on sheet of waxed paper. Using waxed paper to hold dough, roll back and forth to form log about 2½ inches in diameter and 12 inches long. Securely wrap log with plastic wrap. Refrigerate at least 2 hours or until firm. (Log may be frozen up to 3 months; thaw in refrigerator before baking.)

3. Preheat oven to 350°F. Cut dough into ¼-inch-thick slices. Place 2 inches apart on ungreased cookie sheets.

4. Bake 10 minutes or until set. Cool on cookie sheets 2 minutes; remove to wire racks to cool completely.

5. Dip half of each cookie into melted chocolate. Place on waxed paper; let stand at room temperature about 40 minutes or until chocolate is set. Store cookies between sheets of waxed paper at room temperature or in refrigerator.

New England Raisin Spice Cookies

MAKES ABOUT 5 DOZEN COOKIES

2¼ cups all-purpose flour

2 teaspoons baking soda

1 teaspoon salt

¾ teaspoon ground cinnamon

¼ teaspoon ground ginger

¼ teaspoon ground cloves

⅛ teaspoon ground allspice

1½ cups raisins

1 cup packed brown sugar

½ cup shortening

¼ cup (½ stick) butter

1 egg

⅓ cup molasses

1 cup granulated sugar

1. Combine flour, baking soda, salt, cinnamon, ginger, cloves and allspice in medium bowl; mix well. Stir in raisins.

2. Beat brown sugar, shortening and butter in large bowl with electric mixer at medium speed until creamy. Add egg and molasses; beat until light and fluffy. Gradually add flour mixture at low speed, beating just until blended. Cover and refrigerate at least 2 hours.

3. Preheat oven to 350°F. Place granulated sugar in shallow bowl. Shape heaping tablespoonfuls of dough into balls. Roll in granulated sugar to coat. Place 2 inches apart on ungreased cookie sheets.

4. Bake 8 minutes or until golden brown. Cool on cookie sheets 1 minute; remove to wire racks to cool completely.

Chocolate Coconut Toffee Delights

MAKES 1 DOZEN LARGE COOKIES

- 2 **cups semisweet chocolate chips, divided**
- 1/4 **cup (1/2 stick) butter, cut into small pieces**
- 1/2 **cup all-purpose flour**
- 1/4 **teaspoon baking powder**
- 1/4 **teaspoon salt**
- 3/4 **cup packed brown sugar**
- 2 **eggs, lightly beaten**
- 1 **teaspoon vanilla**
- 1 1/2 **cups flaked coconut**
- 1 **cup toffee baking bits**
- 1/2 **cup bittersweet chocolate chips**

1. Preheat oven to 350°F. Line cookie sheets with parchment paper.

2. Place 1 cup semisweet chocolate chips and butter in medium microwavable bowl. Microwave on HIGH 1 minute; stir. Microwave at additional 30-second intervals until mixture is melted and smooth, stirring after each interval.

3. Combine flour, baking powder and salt in small bowl; mix well. Beat brown sugar, eggs and vanilla in large bowl with electric mixer at medium speed until creamy. Beat in chocolate mixture until well blended. Add flour mixture; beat at low speed until blended. Stir in coconut, toffee bits and remaining 1 cup semisweet chocolate chips. Drop dough by heaping 1/3 cupfuls 3 inches apart onto prepared cookie sheets. Flatten into 3 1/2-inch circles with spatula.

4. Bake 15 to 17 minutes or until edges are firm to the touch. Cool on cookie sheets 2 minutes; slide parchment paper and cookies onto wire racks to cool completely.

5. Place bittersweet chocolate chips in small microwavable bowl. Microwave on HIGH 30 seconds; stir. Microwave at additional 30-second intervals until melted and smooth, stirring after each interval. Drizzle chocolate over cookies with fork. Let stand until set.

Pumpkin Whoopie Minis
MAKES ABOUT 2½ DOZEN SANDWICH COOKIES

1¾ cups all-purpose flour

2 teaspoons pumpkin pie spice

1 teaspoon baking powder

1 teaspoon baking soda

1 teaspoon salt, divided

1 cup packed brown sugar

½ cup (1 stick) butter, softened, divided

1 cup canned pumpkin

2 eggs, lightly beaten

¼ cup vegetable oil

1 teaspoon vanilla, divided

4 ounces cream cheese, softened

1½ cups powdered sugar

1. Preheat oven to 350°F. Line cookie sheets with parchment paper.

2. Combine flour, pumpkin pie spice, baking powder, baking soda and ¾ teaspoon salt in medium bowl; mix well. Beat brown sugar and ¼ cup butter in large bowl with electric mixer at medium speed until creamy. Beat in pumpkin, eggs, oil and ½ teaspoon vanilla until well blended. Beat in flour mixture at low speed just until blended. Drop dough by teaspoonfuls 2 inches apart onto prepared cookie sheets.

3. Bake 10 to 12 minutes or until tops spring back when lightly touched. Cool on cookie sheets 5 minutes; remove to wire racks to cool completely.

4. Meanwhile, prepare filling. Beat cream cheese and remaining ¼ cup butter in medium bowl with electric mixer at medium speed until smooth and creamy. Beat in remaining ½ teaspoon vanilla and ¼ teaspoon salt until blended. Gradually add powdered sugar; beat until light and fluffy.

5. Pipe or spread heaping teaspoon filling on flat side of half of cookies; top with remaining cookies. Store cookies in airtight container in refrigerator.

BAR COOKIES

Chocolate Chip Shortbread

MAKES ABOUT 1 DOZEN BARS

- ½ cup (1 stick) butter, softened
- ½ cup granulated sugar
- 2 tablespoons packed brown sugar
- 1 teaspoon vanilla
- 1 cup all-purpose flour
- ½ teaspoon salt
- ½ cup plus 2 tablespoons mini semisweet chocolate chips, divided

1. Preheat oven to 350°F.

2. Beat butter, granulated sugar and brown sugar in large bowl with electric mixer at medium speed until light and fluffy. Beat in vanilla. Add flour and salt; beat at low speed just until combined. Stir in ½ cup chocolate chips.

3. Press dough into 8- or 9-inch square baking pan. Sprinkle with remaining 2 tablespoons chocolate chips; press lightly into dough.

4. Bake 15 to 17 minutes or until edges are golden brown. Cool completely in pan on wire rack. Cut into rectangles or squares.

VARIATION: For shortbread wedges, press dough into 8-inch round baking pan. Bake 14 to 16 minutes or until edge is golden brown and center is set. Cool completely in pan on wire rack; cut into 8 wedges.

Rich Cocoa Brownies

MAKES 2½ DOZEN BROWNIES

2 cups all-purpose flour

2 cups granulated sugar

1 cup (2 sticks) butter

1 cup hot coffee

¼ cup unsweetened cocoa powder

½ cup buttermilk

2 eggs, lightly beaten

1 teaspoon baking soda

1 teaspoon vanilla

Cocoa Frosting (recipe follows)

1. Preheat oven to 400°F. Spray 17½×11-inch jelly-roll pan with nonstick cooking spray.

2. Combine flour and granulated sugar in large bowl; mix well. Combine butter, coffee and cocoa in medium saucepan; bring to a boil over medium heat, stirring constantly. Whisk buttermilk, eggs, baking soda and vanilla in small bowl until blended. Stir cocoa mixture into flour mixture until smooth. Stir in buttermilk mixture until well blended. Pour batter into prepared pan.

3. Bake 20 minutes or until center springs back when touched. Meanwhile, prepare Cocoa Frosting.

4. Remove brownies from oven; immediately pour warm frosting over hot brownies, spreading evenly. Cool in pan on wire rack.

COCOA FROSTING: Combine ½ cup (1 stick) butter, 2 tablespoons unsweetened cocoa powder and ¼ cup milk in large saucepan; bring to a boil over medium heat. Remove from heat; beat in 3½ cups powdered sugar and 1 teaspoon vanilla until smooth.

Pumpkin Cheesecake Bars

MAKES 2 TO 3 DOZEN BARS

1½ **cups gingersnap crumbs,
    plus additional for garnish**

6 **tablespoons butter, melted**

2 **eggs**

¼ **cup plus 2 tablespoons sugar,
   divided**

2½ **teaspoons vanilla, divided**

11 **ounces cream cheese,
    softened**

1¼ **cups canned pumpkin**

1 **teaspoon ground cinnamon**

¼ **teaspoon ground ginger**

¼ **teaspoon ground nutmeg**

¼ **teaspoon ground cloves**

1 **cup sour cream**

1. Preheat oven to 325°F. Spray 13×9-inch baking pan with nonstick cooking spray.

2. Combine 1½ cups gingersnap crumbs and butter in small bowl; mix well. Press into bottom of prepared pan. Bake 10 minutes.

3. Meanwhile, combine eggs, ¼ cup sugar and 1½ teaspoons vanilla in food processor or blender; process 1 minute or until smooth. Add cream cheese and pumpkin; process until well blended. Stir in cinnamon, ginger, nutmeg and cloves. Pour evenly over hot crust.

4. Bake 40 minutes. Whisk sour cream, remaining 2 tablespoons sugar and 1 teaspoon vanilla in small bowl until blended. Remove cheesecake from oven; spread sour cream mixture evenly over top. Bake 5 minutes.

5. Turn oven off; open door halfway and let cheesecake cool completely in oven. Refrigerate at least 2 hours before serving. Garnish with additional gingersnap crumbs.

Seven Layer Bars

MAKES 2 TO 3 DOZEN BARS

½ cup (1 stick) butter, melted

1 teaspoon vanilla

1 cup graham cracker crumbs

1 cup butterscotch chips

1 cup semisweet or milk chocolate chips

1 cup shredded coconut

1 cup nuts

1 can (14 ounces) sweetened condensed milk

1. Preheat oven to 350°F.

2. Pour butter into 13×9-inch baking pan. Add vanilla. Sprinkle graham cracker crumbs over butter; top with butterscotch chips, chocolate chips, coconut and nuts. Pour condensed milk over top.

3. Bake 25 minutes or until lightly browned. Cool completely in pan on wire rack.

VARIATIONS: There are countless ways to change and customize this classic recipe, starting with the chips and nuts. Try white chocolate chips or bittersweet chips if you prefer those flavors, and use whatever nuts you have on hand—pecans, walnuts, almonds, peanuts or a combination. Add a layer of chopped cookies, crushed pretzels or dried cranberries, or swap out the chips for chopped candy bars. For holidays, use colored candy-coated chocolate pieces for a festive look (orange for Halloween, red and green for Christmas, etc.).

bar cookies

Mocha Cinnamon Blondies

MAKES 2 TO 3 DOZEN BLONDIES

1 cup (2 sticks) butter, melted and cooled

1¾ cups sugar

4 eggs

1 cup all-purpose flour

2 teaspoons instant coffee granules

1 teaspoon ground cinnamon

¼ teaspoon salt

1 cup chopped pecans

¾ cup semisweet chocolate chips

1. Preheat oven to 350°F. Spray 13×9-inch baking pan with nonstick cooking spray.

2. Beat butter, sugar and eggs in large bowl with electric mixer at medium speed until light and fluffy. Add flour, coffee granules, cinnamon and salt; beat at low speed until blended. Stir in pecans and chocolate chips. Spread batter in prepared pan.

3. Bake 30 minutes or until edges begin to pull away from sides of pan. Cool completely in pan on wire rack.

Pumpkin Swirl Brownies

MAKES ABOUT 16 BROWNIES

PUMPKIN SWIRL

- **4 ounces cream cheese, softened**
- **1/2 cup canned pumpkin**
- **1 egg**
- **3 tablespoons sugar**
- **3/4 teaspoon pumpkin pie spice**
- **Pinch salt**

BROWNIES

- **1/2 cup (1 stick) butter**
- **6 ounces semisweet chocolate, chopped**
- **1 cup sugar**
- **3 eggs**
- **1 teaspoon vanilla**
- **3/4 cup all-purpose flour**
- **2 tablespoons unsweetened cocoa powder**
- **1/2 teaspoon salt**

1. Preheat oven to 350°F. Spray 8-inch square baking pan with nonstick cooking spray or line with parchment paper.

2. For swirl, combine cream cheese, pumpkin, 1 egg, 3 tablespoons sugar, pumpkin pie spice and pinch of salt in medium bowl; beat until smooth.

3. For brownies, melt butter and chocolate in medium saucepan over low heat, stirring frequently. Remove from heat; stir in 1 cup sugar until blended. Beat in 3 eggs, one at a time, until well blended. Stir in vanilla. Add flour, cocoa and 1/2 teaspoon salt; stir until blended. Reserve 1/3 cup brownie batter in small bowl; spread remaining batter in prepared pan.

4. Spread pumpkin mixture evenly over brownie batter. Drop reserved brownie batter by teaspoonfuls over pumpkin layer; draw tip of knife through top of both batters to marbleize. (If reserved brownie batter has become very thick upon standing, microwave on LOW (30%) 20 to 30 seconds or until loosened, stirring at 10-second intervals.)

5. Bake 28 to 30 minutes or just until center is set and edges begin to pull away from sides of pan. (Toothpick will come out with fudgy crumbs.) Cool in pan on wire rack.

Cranberry Coconut Bars

MAKES 2 TO 3 DOZEN BARS

2 cups fresh or frozen cranberries

1 cup dried sweetened cranberries

²/₃ cup granulated sugar

¹/₄ cup water

Grated peel of 1 lemon

1¹/₄ cups all-purpose flour

³/₄ cup old-fashioned oats

¹/₂ teaspoon baking soda

¹/₂ teaspoon salt

1 cup packed brown sugar

³/₄ cup (1¹/₂ sticks) butter, softened

1 cup shredded sweetened coconut

1 cup chopped pecans, toasted*

*To toast pecans, spread on baking sheet. Bake in preheated 350°F oven 5 to 7 minutes or until lightly browned, stirring frequently.

1. Preheat oven to 400°F. Grease and flour 13×9-inch baking pan.

2. Combine fresh cranberries, dried cranberries, granulated sugar, water and lemon peel in medium saucepan. Cook over medium-high heat 10 to 15 minutes or until cranberries begin to pop, stirring frequently. Mash cranberries with back of spoon. Let stand 10 minutes.

3. Combine flour, oats, baking soda and salt in medium bowl; mix well. Beat brown sugar and butter in large bowl with electric mixer at medium speed until creamy. Add flour mixture; beat just until blended. Stir in coconut and pecans. Reserve 1¹/₂ cups; press remaining crumb mixture into bottom of prepared pan. Bake 10 minutes.

4. Gently spread cranberry filling evenly over crust; sprinkle with reserved crumb mixture. Bake 18 to 20 minutes or until center is set and top is golden brown. Cool completely in pan on wire rack.

NOTE: When fresh or frozen cranberries aren't available, you can make these bars with dried cranberries. Prepare the filling using 2 cups dried sweetened cranberries, 1 cup water and the grated peel of 1 lemon; cook 8 to 10 minutes over medium heat, stirring frequently. Use as directed in step 4.

bar cookies | # Chocolate Dream Bars
MAKES 2 TO 3 DOZEN BARS

2¼ cups all-purpose flour, divided

1 cup (2 sticks) butter, softened

¾ cup powdered sugar, plus additional for garnish

⅓ cup unsweetened cocoa powder

½ teaspoon salt

2 cups granulated sugar

4 eggs, lightly beaten

4 ounces unsweetened chocolate, melted

1. Preheat oven to 350°F. Line 13×9-inch baking pan with parchment paper.

2. Beat 2 cups flour, butter, ¾ cup powdered sugar, cocoa and salt in large bowl with electric mixer at low speed until blended. Beat at medium speed until well blended and stiff dough forms. Press firmly into bottom of prepared pan. Bake 15 to 20 minutes or just until set. *Do not overbake.*

3. Meanwhile, combine remaining ¼ cup flour and granulated sugar in large bowl; mix well. Add eggs and melted chocolate; beat with electric mixer at medium-high speed until well blended. Pour over warm crust.

4. Bake 25 minutes or until center is firm to the touch. Cool completely in pan on wire rack. Sprinkle with additional powdered sugar, if desired.

Sweet Potato Coconut Bars

MAKES 2 TO 3 DOZEN BARS

30 vanilla wafers, crushed (see Tip)

1½ cups finely chopped walnuts, toasted,* divided

1 cup sweetened flaked coconut, divided

¼ cup (½ stick) butter, softened

2 cans (15 ounces each) sweet potatoes, well drained and mashed (2 cups)

2 eggs

1 teaspoon ground cinnamon

½ teaspoon ground ginger

¼ teaspoon salt

¼ teaspoon ground cloves

1 can (14 ounces) sweetened condensed milk

1 cup butterscotch chips

To toast walnuts, spread on baking sheet. Bake in preheated 350°F oven 6 to 8 minutes or until lightly browned, stirring frequently.

1. Preheat oven to 350°F.

2. Combine vanilla wafers, 1 cup walnuts, ½ cup coconut and butter in medium bowl; mix well. (Mixture will be dry and crumbly.) Press two thirds of crumb mixture into bottom of ungreased 13×9-inch baking pan, pressing down lightly to form even layer.

3. Beat mashed sweet potatoes, eggs, cinnamon, ginger, salt and cloves in large bowl with electric mixer at medium-low speed until well blended. Gradually add condensed milk; beat until well blended. Spread filling evenly over crust. Top with remaining crumb mixture, pressing lightly into sweet potato layer.

4. Bake 25 to 30 minutes or until knife inserted into center comes out clean. Sprinkle with butterscotch chips, remaining ½ cup walnuts and ½ cup coconut. Bake 2 minutes. Cool completely in pan on wire rack. Cover and refrigerate 2 hours before serving.

TIP: Vanilla wafers can be crushed in a large food processor or in a resealable food storage bag with a rolling pin or meat mallet.

Shortbread Turtle Cookie Bars

MAKES ABOUT 4½ DOZEN BARS

1¼ cups (2½ sticks) butter, softened, divided

1 cup all-purpose flour

1 cup old-fashioned oats

1¼ cups packed brown sugar, divided

1 teaspoon ground cinnamon

¼ teaspoon salt

1½ cups chopped pecans

6 ounces bittersweet or semisweet chocolate, finely chopped

4 ounces white chocolate, finely chopped

1. Place rack in center of oven. Preheat oven to 350°F.

2. Beat ½ cup butter in large bowl with electric mixer at medium speed 2 minutes or until light and fluffy. Add flour, oats, ¾ cup brown sugar, cinnamon and salt; beat at low speed until coarse crumbs form. Press firmly into bottom of ungreased 13×9-inch baking pan.

3. Combine remaining ¾ cup butter and ¾ cup brown sugar in medium saucepan. Cook over medium heat until mixture comes to a boil, stirring constantly. Boil 1 minute without stirring. Remove from heat; stir in pecans. Pour evenly over crust.

4. Bake 18 to 22 minutes or until caramel begins to bubble. Immediately sprinkle with bittersweet and white chocolate; swirl (do not spread) with knife after 45 seconds to 1 minute or when slightly softened. Cool completely in pan on wire rack.

Toffee Latte Nut Bars

MAKES 2 TO 3 DOZEN BARS

1½ cups all-purpose flour

¼ cup powdered sugar

½ teaspoon salt

¾ cup (1½ sticks) cold butter, cut into pieces

2 teaspoons instant coffee granules

1 teaspoon hot water

1 can (14 ounces) sweetened condensed milk

1 egg

1 teaspoon vanilla

1 package (8 ounces) toffee baking bits

1 cup chopped walnuts or pecans

¾ cup flaked coconut *or* 1 cup large coconut flakes

1. Preheat oven to 350°F. Line 13×9-inch pan with parchment paper or spray with nonstick cooking spray.

2. Combine flour, powdered sugar and salt in large bowl; mix well. Cut in butter with pastry blender or two knives until mixture resembles coarse crumbs. Press into bottom of prepared pan. Bake 15 minutes or until lightly browned around edges.

3. Meanwhile, dissolve coffee granules in hot water in small bowl. Pour condensed milk into medium bowl; stir in coffee mixture. Beat in egg and vanilla until well blended. Stir in toffee bits and walnuts. Pour over warm crust; sprinkle with coconut.

4. Bake 25 minutes or until filling is set and coconut is toasted. Cool 5 minutes, then loosen edges by running knife around sides of pan. Cool completely in pan on wire rack. Lift from pan using parchment; cut into bars.

Key Lime Bars

MAKES 2 TO 3 DOZEN BARS

1½ **cups finely crushed graham crackers (10 to 12 crackers)**

4 **tablespoons packed brown sugar**

2 **tablespoons all-purpose flour**

5 **tablespoons melted butter**

1 **package (8 ounces) cream cheese, softened**

1½ **cups granulated sugar**

2 **eggs**

¼ **cup Key lime juice**

1 **tablespoon grated lime peel**
  Lime slices (optional)

1. Place rack in center of oven. Preheat oven to 350°F. Spray 13×9-inch baking pan with nonstick cooking spray.

2. Combine graham cracker crumbs, brown sugar and flour in large bowl; mix well. Gradually add butter, stirring until mixture is thoroughly moist and crumbly. Press into bottom of prepared pan. Bake 15 minutes.

3. Meanwhile, beat cream cheese and granulated sugar in large bowl with electric mixer at medium speed until smooth and creamy. Add eggs, one at a time, beating well after each addition. Add lime juice and lime peel; beat just until blended. Pour over warm crust.

4. Bake 15 to 20 minutes or until filling is set and begins to pull away from sides of pan.

5. Cool on wire rack 2 hours. Garnish with lime slices.

Celebration Brownies
MAKES 2 TO 3 DOZEN BROWNIES

1 cup (2 sticks) butter

8 ounces semisweet baking chocolate, coarsely chopped

1 cup sugar

4 eggs

1 teaspoon vanilla

1 teaspoon salt

1¼ cups all-purpose flour

2 cups dark or semisweet chocolate chips, divided

¼ cup whipping cream

1 container (about 2 ounces) rainbow nonpareils

1. Preheat oven to 350°F. Spray 13×9-inch baking pan with nonstick cooking spray or line with parchment paper.

2. Heat butter and chocolate in large saucepan over low heat; stir until melted and smooth. Remove from heat; stir in sugar until blended. Add eggs, one at a time, stirring until well blended after each addition. Stir in vanilla and salt. Add flour and 1 cup chocolate chips; stir just until blended. Spread batter evenly in prepared pan.

3. Bake 22 to 25 minutes or until center is set and toothpick inserted into center comes out clean. Cool completely in pan on wire rack.

4. Heat cream in small saucepan over medium-low heat until bubbles appear around edge of pan. Remove from heat; add remaining 1 cup chocolate chips. Let stand 1 minute; whisk until smooth and well blended. Spread evenly over brownies; top with nonpareils.

Whole Wheat Pumpkin Bars

MAKES 2 TO 3 DOZEN BARS

1 cup all-purpose flour

1 cup whole wheat flour

¾ cup sugar

1½ teaspoons baking powder

1½ teaspoons ground cinnamon

1 teaspoon baking soda

¾ teaspoon salt

½ teaspoon ground ginger

½ teaspoon ground nutmeg

1 can (15 ounces) solid-pack pumpkin

¾ cup vegetable or canola oil

2 eggs

2 tablespoons molasses

Cream Cheese Frosting (recipe follows)

½ cup mini semisweet chocolate chips

1. Preheat oven to 350°F. Spray 13×9-inch baking pan with nonstick cooking spray.

2. Combine all-purpose flour, whole wheat flour, sugar, baking powder, cinnamon, baking soda, salt, ginger and nutmeg in medium bowl; mix well. Whisk pumpkin, oil, eggs and molasses in large bowl until well blended. Add flour mixture; stir until blended. Spread batter in prepared pan. (Batter will be very thick.)

3. Bake 20 to 25 minutes or until toothpick inserted into center comes out clean. Cool completely in pan on wire rack.

4. Prepare Cream Cheese Frosting. Spread frosting over bars; sprinkle with chocolate chips.

CREAM CHEESE FROSTING: Beat 4 ounces softened cream cheese and ½ cup (1 stick) softened butter in medium bowl with electric mixer at medium-high speed until creamy. Add 2 cups powdered sugar; beat at low speed until blended. Add 1 tablespoon milk; beat at medium-high speed 2 to 3 minutes or until frosting is light and fluffy.

Honey Nut Granola Bars

MAKES 16 BARS

½ cup (1 stick) butter

½ cup honey

¼ cup packed brown sugar

¼ cup corn syrup

2¾ cups quick oats

⅔ cup raisins

½ cup salted peanuts

1. Preheat oven to 300°F. Spray 9-inch square baking pan with nonstick cooking spray.

2. Melt butter, honey, brown sugar and corn syrup in large saucepan over medium heat, stirring constantly. Bring to a boil; boil 8 minutes or until mixture thickens slightly. Stir in oats, raisins and peanuts until well blended. Press evenly into prepared pan.

3. Bake 25 to 30 minutes or until golden brown. Score into 2-inch squares. Cool completely in pan on wire rack. Cut into bars along score lines.

Chocolate Chip Brownies

MAKES 16 BROWNIES

3/4 **cup granulated sugar**

1/2 **cup (1 stick) butter**

2 **tablespoons water**

2 **cups semisweet chocolate chips or mini chocolate chips, divided**

1 1/2 **teaspoons vanilla**

1 1/4 **cups all-purpose flour**

1/2 **teaspoon baking soda**

1/2 **teaspoon salt**

2 **eggs**

Powdered sugar (optional)

1. Preheat oven to 350°F. Spray 9-inch square baking pan with nonstick cooking spray.

2. Combine granulated sugar, butter and water in medium microwavable bowl; microwave on HIGH 1 1/2 to 2 minutes or until butter is melted. Stir in 1 cup chocolate chips; stir until chips are melted and mixture is smooth. Stir in vanilla; let stand 5 minutes.

3. Combine flour, baking soda and salt in small bowl; mix well. Add eggs to chocolate mixture, one at a time, beating well after each addition. Add flour mixture; stir until blended. Stir in remaining 1 cup chocolate chips. Spread batter evenly in prepared pan.

4. Bake 25 minutes for fudgy brownies or 30 to 35 minutes for cakelike brownies. Cool completely in pan on wire rack. Sprinkle with powdered sugar, if desired.

DESSERTS

Black Forest Cobbler

MAKES 8 TO 10 SERVINGS

FILLING

- 3 **pounds frozen pitted sweet cherries, thawed and drained**
- ³/₄ **cup sugar**
- ¹/₄ **cup cornstarch**
- 2 **tablespoons lemon juice**
- 1 **teaspoon vanilla**

BISCUIT TOPPING

- 1¹/₄ **cups all-purpose flour**
- ¹/₂ **cup sugar**
- ¹/₄ **cup unsweetened cocoa powder**
- 1¹/₂ **teaspoons baking powder**
- 1 **teaspoon baking soda**
- ¹/₂ **teaspoon salt**
- 6 **tablespoons (³/₄ stick) butter, cut into small pieces**
- ¹/₂ **cup semisweet chocolate chips**
- ²/₃ **cup buttermilk**

1. Preheat oven to 375°F. Spray 9-inch square baking pan with nonstick cooking spray.

2. For filling, combine cherries, ³/₄ cup sugar, cornstarch, lemon juice and vanilla in large bowl; toss to coat. Spoon into prepared pan.

3. For topping, combine flour, ¹/₂ cup sugar, cocoa, baking powder, baking soda and salt in medium bowl; mix well. Cut in butter with pastry blender or mix with fingertips until mixture resembles coarse crumbs. Stir in chocolate chips. Add buttermilk; stir just until combined. *Do not overmix.* Drop topping, 2 tablespoonfuls at a time, into mounds over cherry mixture.

4. Bake 40 to 45 minutes or until filling is bubbly and toothpick inserted into center of biscuit comes out clean. Let stand 30 minutes before serving. Serve warm.

Pumpkin Bread Pudding

MAKES 2 SERVINGS

2 slices whole wheat bread

1 cup canned pumpkin

1 egg

2 tablespoons sugar

1 teaspoon vanilla

½ teaspoon ground cinnamon, plus additional for garnish

1 tablespoon raisins

Whipped cream (optional)

1. Preheat oven to 375°F. Spray two ovenproof custard cups or ramekins with nonstick cooking spray.

2. Toast bread; cut into 1-inch cubes.

3. Whisk pumpkin, egg, sugar, vanilla and ½ teaspoon cinnamon in medium bowl until well blended. Fold in toasted bread cubes and raisins. Divide mixture evenly between prepared cups.

4. Bake 30 minutes. Serve warm with whipped cream, if desired. Garnish with additional cinnamon.

Apple Cranberry Crumble

MAKES 4 SERVINGS

4 large apples (about 1¹/₃ pounds), peeled and cut into ¹/₄-inch slices

2 cups fresh or frozen cranberries

¹/₃ cup granulated sugar

6 tablespoons all-purpose flour, divided

1 teaspoon apple pie spice, divided

¹/₄ teaspoon salt, divided

¹/₂ cup chopped walnuts

¹/₄ cup old-fashioned oats

2 tablespoons packed brown sugar

¹/₄ cup (¹/₂ stick) butter, cut into small pieces

1. Preheat oven to 375°F.

2. Combine apples, cranberries, granulated sugar, 2 tablespoons flour, ¹/₂ teaspoon apple pie spice and ¹/₈ teaspoon salt in large bowl; toss to coat. Spoon into medium (8-inch) cast iron skillet.

3. Combine remaining 4 tablespoons flour, walnuts, oats, brown sugar, remaining ¹/₂ teaspoon apple pie spice and ¹/₈ teaspoon salt in medium bowl; mix well. Cut in butter with pastry blender or two knives until mixture resembles coarse crumbs. Sprinkle over fruit mixture in skillet.

4. Bake 50 to 60 minutes or until filling is bubbly and topping is lightly browned.

Bananas Foster Crisp

MAKES 8 TO 10 SERVINGS

¾ **cup packed dark brown sugar, divided**

6 **tablespoons (¾ stick) butter, divided**

3 **tablespoons dark rum**

½ **teaspoon ground cinnamon**

¼ **teaspoon grated nutmeg**

8 **medium bananas (firm, yellow, no spots), cut into ½-inch slices (about 6 cups)**

½ **cup all-purpose flour**

½ **cup chopped pecans**

¼ **teaspoon salt**

Vanilla ice cream (optional)

1. Place oven rack in lower-middle position. Preheat oven to 375°F. Spray 8-inch round or square baking dish with nonstick cooking spray.

2. Combine ½ cup brown sugar and 2 tablespoons butter in small saucepan; cook and stir over medium heat about 3 minutes or until butter is melted and sugar is dissolved. Slowly add rum, cinnamon and nutmeg (mixture will spatter); cook 1 minute, stirring constantly. Pour mixture into large bowl. Add bananas; toss to coat. Spoon into prepared baking dish.

3. Combine flour, pecans, remaining ¼ cup brown sugar and salt in medium bowl; mix well. Cut remaining 4 tablespoons butter into small pieces. Add to flour mixture; mix with fingertips until mixture forms coarse crumbs. Sprinkle over banana mixture.

4. Bake 40 minutes or until filling is bubbly and topping is golden brown. Let stand 1 hour before serving. Serve with ice cream, if desired.

Baklava

MAKES ABOUT 32 PIECES

4 cups walnuts, shelled pistachio nuts and/or slivered almonds (1 pound)

1¼ cups sugar, divided

2 teaspoons ground cinnamon

¼ teaspoon ground cloves

1 cup (2 sticks) butter, melted

1 package (16 ounces) frozen phyllo dough (about 20 sheets), thawed

1½ cups water

¾ cup honey

2 (2-inch-long) strips lemon peel

1 tablespoon lemon juice

1 cinnamon stick

3 whole cloves

1. Place half of walnuts in food processor. Pulse until nuts are finely chopped but not pasty. Transfer to large bowl; repeat with remaining nuts. Add ½ cup sugar, ground cinnamon and ground cloves to nuts; mix well.

2. Preheat oven to 325°F. Brush 13×9-inch baking dish with some of melted butter or line with foil, leaving overhang on two sides for easy removal. Unroll phyllo dough and place on large sheet of waxed paper. Trim phyllo sheets to 13×9 inches. Cover phyllo with plastic wrap and damp, clean kitchen towel to prevent drying out.

3. Place 1 phyllo sheet in bottom of dish, folding in edges if too long; brush with butter. Repeat with 7 additional phyllo sheets, brushing each sheet with butter as it is layered. Sprinkle with ½ cup nut mixture; top with 3 additional layers of phyllo, brushing each sheet with butter. Sprinkle with ½ cup nut mixture. Repeat layering and brushing of 3 phyllo sheets with ½ cup nut mixture until there is a total of eight layers. Top final layer of nut mixture with remaining phyllo sheets, brushing each sheet with butter.

4. Score baklava lengthwise into 4 equal sections, then cut diagonally at 1½-inch intervals to form diamond shapes. Sprinkle top lightly with water to prevent top phyllo layers from curling up during baking.

5. Bake 50 to 60 minutes or until golden brown. Meanwhile, prepare syrup. Combine 1½ cups water, remaining ¾ cup sugar, honey, lemon peel, lemon juice, cinnamon stick and whole cloves in medium saucepan; bring to a boil over high heat. Reduce heat to low; simmer 15 minutes. Strain hot syrup; drizzle evenly over hot baklava. Cool completely in pan on wire rack. Cut into pieces along score lines.

Ginger Pear Cobbler

MAKES 8 TO 10 SERVINGS

7 firm ripe d'Anjou pears (about 3½ pounds), peeled and cut into ½-inch pieces

⅓ cup packed brown sugar

1 cup plus 2 tablespoons all-purpose flour, divided

2 tablespoons lemon juice

2 teaspoons ground ginger, divided

½ teaspoon ground cinnamon

⅛ teaspoon ground nutmeg

¼ cup granulated sugar, divided

1½ teaspoons baking powder

¼ teaspoon salt

¼ cup (½ stick) butter, cut into small pieces

¼ cup whipping cream

1 egg, lightly beaten

1 tablespoon sparkling sugar (optional)

1. Preheat oven to 375°F. Spray 9-inch square baking dish with nonstick cooking spray.

2. Combine pears, brown sugar, 2 tablespoons flour, lemon juice, 1 teaspoon ginger, cinnamon and nutmeg in large bowl; toss to coat. Spoon into prepared baking dish.

3. Combine remaining 1 cup flour, 1 teaspoon ginger, granulated sugar, baking powder and salt in medium bowl; mix well. Add butter; mix with fingertips until shaggy clumps form. Add cream and egg; stir just until combined. Drop topping, 2 tablespoonfuls at a time, into mounds over pear mixture. Sprinkle with sparkling sugar, if desired.

4. Bake 40 to 45 minutes or until filling is bubbly and topping is golden brown.

Chocolate Crème Brûlée

MAKES 4 SERVINGS

2 **cups whipping cream**

3 **ounces semisweet or bittersweet baking chocolate, finely chopped**

3 **egg yolks**

¼ **cup granulated sugar**

2 **teaspoons vanilla**

3 **tablespoons packed brown sugar**

1. Preheat oven to 325°F. Heat cream in medium saucepan over medium heat until it just begins to simmer. *Do not boil.* Remove from heat; stir in chocolate until melted and smooth. Set aside to cool slightly.

2. Beat egg yolks and granulated sugar in large bowl with electric mixer at medium-high speed 5 minutes or until thick and pale yellow. Beat in chocolate mixture and vanilla until blended.

3. Divide mixture evenly among four 6-ounce custard cups or individual baking dishes. Place cups in baking pan; place pan in oven. Pour boiling water into baking pan to reach halfway up sides of custard cups. Cover pan loosely with foil.

4. Bake 30 minutes or just until edges are set. Remove cups from baking pan to wire rack to cool completely. Cover with plastic wrap; refrigerate 4 hours or up to 3 days.

5. When ready to serve, preheat broiler. Spread about 2 teaspoons brown sugar evenly over each cup. Broil 3 to 4 minutes or until sugar bubbles and browns. Serve immediately.

desserts | # Plum Rhubarb Crumble

MAKES 6 TO 8 SERVINGS

1½ **pounds plums, each pitted and cut into 8 wedges (4 cups)**

1½ **pounds rhubarb, cut into ½-inch pieces (5 cups)**

1 **cup granulated sugar**

1 **teaspoon finely grated fresh ginger**

¼ **teaspoon ground nutmeg**

3 **tablespoons cornstarch**

¾ **cup old-fashioned oats**

½ **cup all-purpose flour**

½ **cup packed brown sugar**

½ **cup sliced almonds, toasted***

¼ **teaspoon salt**

½ **cup (1 stick) cold butter, cut into small pieces**

*To toast almonds, spread on baking sheet. Bake in preheated 350°F oven 4 to 6 minutes or until golden brown, stirring frequently.

1. Combine plums, rhubarb, granulated sugar, ginger and nutmeg in large bowl; toss to coat. Cover and let stand at room temperature 2 hours.

2. Preheat oven to 375°F. Spray 9-inch round or square baking dish with nonstick cooking spray. Line baking sheet with foil.

3. Pour juices from fruit mixture into small saucepan; bring to a boil over medium-high heat. Cook about 12 minutes or until reduced to syrupy consistency, stirring occasionally.* Stir in cornstarch until well blended. Stir mixture into bowl with fruit; pour into prepared baking dish.

4. Combine oats, flour, brown sugar, almonds and salt in medium bowl; mix well. Add butter; mix with fingertips until butter is evenly distributed and mixture is clumpy. Sprinkle over fruit mixture. Place baking dish on prepared baking sheet.

5. Bake about 50 minutes or until filling is bubbly and topping is golden brown. Cool 1 hour before serving.

*If fruit is not juicy after 2 hours, liquid will take less time to reduce and require less cornstarch to thicken.

Classic Flan

MAKES 6 SERVINGS

1½ **cups sugar, divided**
 1 **tablespoon water**
¼ **teaspoon ground cinnamon**
 3 **cups whole milk**
 3 **eggs**
 3 **egg yolks**
 1 **teaspoon vanilla**

1. Preheat oven to 300°F.

2. Combine 1 cup sugar, water and cinnamon in medium saucepan; cook over medium-high heat without stirring about 10 minutes or until sugar is melted and mixture is deep golden amber in color. Pour into six 6-ounce ramekins, swirling to coat bottoms. Place ramekins in 13×9-inch baking pan.

3. Heat milk in separate medium saucepan over medium heat until bubbles begin to form around edge of pan.

4. Meanwhile, whisk eggs, egg yolks, vanilla and remaining ½ cup sugar in medium bowl until well blended. Whisk in ½ cup hot milk in thin, steady stream. Gradually whisk in remaining milk. Divide milk mixture evenly among prepared ramekins. Carefully add hot water to baking pan until water comes halfway up sides of ramekins. Cover ramekins with waxed paper or parchment paper.

5. Bake 1 hour 15 minutes or until custard is firm and knife inserted into custard comes out clean. Remove ramekins from baking pan to wire rack; cool completely. Cover and refrigerate until cold. Run small knife around edges of ramekins to loosen; invert flans onto serving plates.

Coconut Cherry Cobbler for a Crowd

MAKES 16 SERVINGS

2 packages (12 ounces each) frozen dark sweet cherries, thawed and juice reserved

1 cup water

1 tablespoon lemon juice

2 teaspoons almond extract

2 cups sugar, divided

1/4 cup cornstarch

3/4 teaspoon salt, divided

3 cups all-purpose flour

1 cup toasted coconut*

1 1/2 teaspoons baking powder

1 cup (2 sticks) butter, softened

4 eggs

To toast coconut, spread on baking sheet. Bake in preheated 350°F oven 8 to 10 minutes or until lightly browned, stirring occasionally.

1. Preheat oven to 350°F. Spray 15×10×1-inch jelly-roll pan with nonstick cooking spray.

2. Combine cherries with juice, water, lemon juice and almond extract in large saucepan. Stir in 3/4 cup sugar, cornstarch and 1/4 teaspoon salt; bring to a boil over medium-high heat. Cook and stir about 2 minutes or until thickened.

3. Combine flour, coconut, baking powder and remaining 1/2 teaspoon salt in medium bowl; mix well. Beat butter and remaining 1 1/4 cups sugar in large bowl with electric mixer at medium speed until light and fluffy. Add eggs; beat until well blended. Beat in flour mixture at low speed just until blended.

4. Reserve 1 1/4 cups dough for topping. Spread remaining dough on bottom of prepared pan using wax paper sprayed with cooking spray. (Dough will be thick and sticky). Spread cherry mixture evenly over dough. Crumble remaining dough over cherries.

5. Bake 35 to 40 minutes or until crust is golden brown. Cool slightly before serving.

Individual Chocolate Soufflés

MAKES 2 SERVINGS

1 **teaspoon butter, divided**

5 **tablespoons granulated sugar, divided**

4 **ounces semisweet chocolate, chopped**

2 **ounces cream cheese, softened**

2 **tablespoons milk**

2 **eggs, separated, at room temperature**

Pinch salt

Powdered sugar

1. Use $1/2$ teaspoon butter to grease two 10-ounce custard cups. Add 1 tablespoon granulated sugar; shake to coat bottoms and sides of cups.

2. To make collars for custard cups, fold 16-inch-long piece of foil in half lengthwise, then fold in half again. Use $1/4$ teaspoon butter to grease half of it lengthwise. Sprinkle buttered part with $1^{1}/_{2}$ teaspoons granulated sugar. Wrap foil around custard cup, buttered side in; allow buttered half to extend above rim by 1 inch. Secure with masking tape if necessary. Repeat for second collar.

3. Preheat oven to 350°F. Place baking pan in oven. Combine chocolate, cream cheese and milk in medium microwavable bowl. Microwave on HIGH 1 minute; stir until smooth. If mixture is not completely melted, microwave at additional 30-second intervals, stirring after each. Cool slightly, then stir in egg yolks until well blended.

4. Beat egg whites in medium bowl with electric mixer at high speed until frothy. Add salt, then gradually add remaining 3 tablespoons granulated sugar, beating until stiff peaks form.

5. Gently fold chocolate mixture into egg whites in three additions. Divide batter between custard cups. Place custard cups in preheated baking pan.

6. Bake 35 to 40 minutes or until soufflés are puffed and toothpick inserted into centers comes out clean. Remove collars; sprinkle with powdered sugar. Serve immediately. (Soufflés deflate as they cool.)

TIP: The soufflés can be prepared in advance: Wrap and refrigerate the soufflés after pouring the batter into the custard cups. (Add the collars after removing the soufflés from the refrigerator.) To bake chilled soufflés, add a few minutes to the baking time.

Dark Chocolate Raspberry Bread Pudding

MAKES 6 TO 8 SERVINGS

8 slices multigrain, wheat or egg bread, cut into ½-inch cubes

¼ cup (½ stick) butter, melted

2 cups whole milk

4 eggs

¾ cup sugar

1 teaspoon vanilla

½ cup fresh raspberries

½ cup bittersweet or semisweet chocolate chips

1. Spray 9-inch square baking dish with nonstick cooking spray.

2. Combine bread cubes and butter in prepared baking dish; toss to coat. Whisk milk, eggs, sugar and vanilla in medium bowl until well blended. Pour over bread cubes; cover and refrigerate 2 hours.

3. Preheat oven to 350°F. Sprinkle raspberries and chocolate chips over bread mixture.

4. Bake 40 to 50 minutes or until golden brown and center is set. Let stand 10 minutes before serving.

Blueberry Lemon Cornmeal Cobbler

MAKES 8 TO 10 SERVINGS

5 cups fresh blueberries

1/2 cup plus 1/3 cup sugar, divided

3 tablespoons lemon juice, divided

2 tablespoons cornstarch

1 1/2 tablespoons finely grated lemon peel, divided

3/4 cup all-purpose flour

1/4 cup fine-ground cornmeal

1 1/2 teaspoons baking powder

1/4 teaspoon salt

1/2 cup buttermilk

1/4 cup (1/2 stick) butter, melted and cooled

1 egg, lightly beaten

1. Preheat oven to 375°F. Spray 8-inch square baking dish with nonstick cooking spray.

2. Combine blueberries, 1/3 cup sugar, 1 tablespoon lemon juice, cornstarch and 1/2 tablespoon lemon peel in large bowl; toss to coat. Spoon into prepared baking dish.

3. Combine flour, cornmeal, remaining 1/2 cup sugar, 1 tablespoon lemon peel, baking powder and salt in medium bowl; mix well. Add buttermilk, butter, egg and remaining 2 tablespoons lemon juice; stir just until combined. Drop topping, 2 tablespoonfuls at a time, into mounds over blueberry mixture.

4. Bake 40 to 45 minutes or until filling is bubbly and topping is golden brown. Let stand 30 minutes before serving.

Perfect Peanut Butter Pudding

MAKES 6 SERVINGS

2 cups milk

2 eggs

⅓ cup creamy peanut butter

¼ cup packed brown sugar

¼ teaspoon vanilla

¾ cup shaved chocolate or shredded coconut (optional)

1. Preheat oven to 350°F. Grease six 3-ounce ovenproof custard cups.

2. Combine milk, eggs, peanut butter, brown sugar and vanilla in blender; blend at high 1 minute. Pour into prepared custard cups. Place cups in 13×9-inch baking pan; carefully add enough hot water to baking pan to come halfway up sides of custard cups.

3. Bake 50 minutes or until pudding is set. Remove custard cups from pan; cool to room temperature. Refrigerate until ready to serve.

4. Just before serving, top each pudding with about 2 tablespoons shaved chocolate, if desired.

A

Almond Glaze, 91
Almonds
    Almond Glaze, 91
    Cherry, Almond and
        Chocolate Twist, 90
    Plum Rhubarb Crumble, 174
    Very Berry Tart, 46
Angel Food Cake, 12
Apple
    Apple Cranberry Crumble, 164
    Apple Glaze, 22
    Classic Apple Pie, 52
    Glazed Applesauce Spice
        Cake, 22
    Swedish Apple Pie, 44
    Warm Apple Crostata, 60
Apple Cranberry Crumble, 164
Apple Glaze, 22

B

Bacon Cheddar Monkey Bread,
    94
Baklava, 168
Banana
    Banana Cake, 34
    Bananas Foster Crisp, 166
    Date-Nut Banana Braid, 74
Banana Cake, 34
Bananas Foster Crisp, 166
Beer Pretzels, 88
Bittersweet Chocolate Tarts,
    38
Black and White Cookies, 108
Black Forest Cobbler, 161
Blueberry
    Blueberry Crumb Cake, 24
    Blueberry Lemon Cornmeal
        Cobbler, 184
    Very Berry Tart, 46
Blueberry Crumb Cake, 24
Blueberry Lemon Cornmeal
    Cobbler, 184
Boston Black Coffee Bread, 68
Breads, Quick
    Boston Black Coffee Bread,
        68
    Cheddar Biscuits, 78

Breads, Quick (*continued*)
    Oat and Whole Wheat
        Scones, 92
    Peanut Butter Bran Muffins,
        86
    Simple Golden Cornbread, 65
    Treacle Bread (Brown Soda
        Bread), 72
Breads, Yeast
    Bacon Cheddar Monkey
        Bread, 94
    Beer Pretzels, 88
    Cardamom Rolls, 66
    Cherry, Almond and
        Chocolate Twist, 90
    Cranberry Brie Bubble Braid,
        76
    Date-Nut Banana Braid, 74
    Focaccia, 70
    Garlic Knots, 84
    Pumpkin Cinnamon Rolls, 82
    Three-Grain Bread, 80
Brownies
    Celebration Brownies, 152
    Chocolate Chip Brownies, 158
    Pumpkin Swirl Brownies, 138
    Rich Cocoa Brownies, 130
Butterscotch
    Butterscotch Malt Zucchini
        Cake, 14
    Glazed Applesauce Spice
        Cake, 22
    Seven Layer Bars, 134
    Sweet Potato Coconut Bars,
        144
    Toffee Cake with Whiskey
        Sauce, 20
Butterscotch Malt Zucchini
    Cake, 14

C

Cakes
    Peanut Butter Cupcakes, 30
    Toffee Cake with Whiskey
        Sauce, 20
Cakes, 13x9
    Chocolate Sheet Cake, 16
    Oat Apricot Snack Cake, 8

Cakes, Bundt & Tube
    Angel Food Cake, 12
    Butterscotch Malt Zucchini
        Cake, 14
    Glazed Applesauce Spice
        Cake, 22
    Pear Spice Cake, 32
Cakes, Layer
    Banana Cake, 34
    Carrot Cake, 26
    Classic Chocolate Birthday
        Cake, 6
    Red Velvet Cake, 18
Cardamom Rolls, 66
Carrot Cake, 26
Celebration Brownies, 152
Cheddar Biscuits, 78
Cheesecake
    Pumpkin Cheesecake, 28
    Pumpkin Cheesecake Bars,
        132
    Turtle Cheesecake, 10
Cherry
    Black Forest Cobbler, 161
    Cherry, Almond and
        Chocolate Twist, 90
    Coconut Cherry Cobbler for
        a Crowd, 178
    Lattice-Topped Cherry Pie,
        48
    Oat and Whole Wheat
        Scones, 92
Cherry, Almond and Chocolate
    Twist, 90
Chocolate
    Banana Cake, 34
    Bittersweet Chocolate Tarts,
        38
    Black and White Cookies, 108
    Black Forest Cobbler, 161
    Celebration Brownies, 152
    Cherry, Almond and
        Chocolate Twist, 90
    Chocolate Chip Brownies,
        158
    Chocolate Chip Sandwich
        Cookies, 112
    Chocolate Chip Shortbread,
        129

Chocolate (*continued*)
Chocolate Coconut Toffee Delights, 124
Chocolate Cookie Pops, 116
Chocolate Crème Brûlée, 172
Chocolate-Dipped Cinnamon Thins, 120
Chocolate Dream Bars, 142
Chocolate Hazelnut Sandwich Cookies, 102
Chocolate Sheet Cake, 16
Chocolate Walnut Toffee Tart, 50
Classic Chocolate Birthday Cake, 6
Cocoa Frosting, 130
Dark Chocolate Raspberry Bread Pudding, 182
Individual Chocolate Soufflés, 180
Marshmallow Sandwich Cookies, 98
Mocha Cinnamon Blondies, 136
Peanut Butter Cupcakes, 30
Peanutty Double Chip Cookies, 106
Perfect Peanut Butter Pudding, 186
Pumpkin Swirl Brownies, 138
Rich Cocoa Brownies, 130
Seven Layer Bars, 134
Shortbread Turtle Cookie Bars, 146
Turtle Cheesecake, 10
Whole Wheat Pumpkin Bars, 154
Chocolate Chip Brownies, 158
Chocolate Chip Sandwich Cookies, 112
Chocolate Chip Shortbread, 129
Chocolate Coconut Toffee Delights, 124
Chocolate Cookie Pops, 116
Chocolate Crème Brûlée, 172
Chocolate-Dipped Cinnamon Thins, 120
Chocolate Dream Bars, 142
Chocolate Hazelnut Sandwich Cookies, 102

Chocolate (*continued*)
Chocolate Sheet Cake, 16
Chocolate Walnut Toffee Tart, 50
Classic Apple Pie, 52
Classic Chocolate Birthday Cake, 6
Classic Flan, 176
Cobblers, Crisps & Crumbles
Apple Cranberry Crumble, 164
Bananas Foster Crisp, 166
Black Forest Cobbler, 161
Blueberry Lemon Cornmeal Cobbler, 184
Coconut Cherry Cobbler for a Crowd, 178
Ginger Pear Cobbler, 170
Plum Rhubarb Crumble, 174
Cocoa Frosting, 130
Coconut
Carrot Cake, 26
Chocolate Coconut Toffee Delights, 124
Coconut Cherry Cobbler for a Crowd, 178
Coconut Meringue Pie, 62
Cranberry Coconut Bars, 140
Seven Layer Bars, 134
Sweet Potato Coconut Bars, 144
Toffee Latte Nut Bars, 148
Coconut Cherry Cobbler for a Crowd, 178
Coconut Meringue Pie, 62
Coffeecakes
Blueberry Crumb Cake, 24
Cherry, Almond and Chocolate Twist, 90
Pumpkin Streusel Coffeecake, 5
Cookies, Bar
Chocolate Chip Shortbread, 129
Chocolate Dream Bars, 142
Cranberry Coconut Bars, 140
Honey Nut Granola Bars, 156
Key Lime Bars, 150
Mocha Cinnamon Blondies, 136

Cookies, Bar (*continued*)
Pumpkin Cheesecake Bars, 132
Seven Layer Bars, 134
Shortbread Turtle Cookie Bars, 146
Sweet Potato Coconut Bars, 144
Toffee Latte Nut Bars, 148
Whole Wheat Pumpkin Bars, 154
Cookies, Cut-Out: Lemony Butter Cookies, 97
Cookies, Drop
Chocolate Chip Sandwich Cookies, 112
Chocolate Coconut Toffee Delights, 124
Chocolate Cookie Pops, 116
PB and J Thumbprint Cookies, 114
Peanutty Double Chip Cookies, 106
Cookies, Refrigerator
Chocolate-Dipped Cinnamon Thins, 120
Chocolate Hazelnut Sandwich Cookies, 102
Gingery Oat and Molasses Cookies, 110
Refrigerator Cookies, 104
Cookies, Sandwich
Chocolate Chip Sandwich Cookies, 112
Chocolate Hazelnut Sandwich Cookies, 102
Marshmallow Sandwich Cookies, 98
Pumpkin Whoopie Minis, 126
Raspberry Macarons, 118
Cookies, Shaped
Black and White Cookies, 108
Marshmallow Sandwich Cookies, 98
New England Raisin Spice Cookies, 122
Snickerdoodles, 100

Cornmeal
Blueberry Lemon Cornmeal
Cobbler, 184
Boston Black Coffee Bread, 68
Simple Golden Cornbread, 65
Three-Grain Bread, 80
Cranberry
Apple Cranberry Crumble, 164
Cranberry Brie Bubble Bread,
76
Cranberry Coconut Bars, 140
Rustic Cranberry-Pear
Galette, 40
Cranberry Brie Bubble Bread, 76
Cranberry Coconut Bars, 140
Cream Cheese
Carrot Cake, 26
Cream Cheese Frosting, 154
Individual Chocolate Soufflés,
180
Key Lime Bars, 150
Pumpkin Cheesecake, 28
Pumpkin Cheesecake Bars,
132
Pumpkin Cinnamon Rolls, 82
Pumpkin Swirl Brownies, 138
Pumpkin Whoopie Minis, 126
Red Velvet Cake, 18
Turtle Cheesecake, 10
Whole Wheat Pumpkin Bars,
154
Cream Cheese Frosting, 154
Crumb Topping, 24

D
Dark Chocolate Raspberry
Bread Pudding, 182
Date-Nut Banana Braid, 74
Double-Crust Pie Pastry, 54

F
Focaccia, 70
Frostings & Glazes
Almond Glaze, 91
Apple Glaze, 22
Cocoa Frosting, 130
Cream Cheese Frosting, 154
Peanut Buttery Frosting, 30

G
Garlic Knots, 84
Ginger Pear Cobbler, 170
Gingery Oat and Molasses
Cookies, 110
Glazed Applesauce Spice Cake,
22

H
Honey Butter, 65
Honey Nut Granola Bars, 156

I
Individual Chocolate Soufflés,
180

K
Key Lime Bars, 150

L
Lattice-Topped Cherry Pie, 48
Lemon
Blueberry Lemon Cornmeal
Cobbler, 184
Lemon Tart, 42
Lemony Butter Cookies, 97
Lemon Tart, 42
Lemony Butter Cookies, 97

M
Marshmallow Sandwich Cookies,
98
Mocha Cinnamon Blondies,
136

N
New England Raisin Spice
Cookies, 122

O
Oat and Whole Wheat Scones,
92
Oat Apricot Snack Cake, 8
Oats
Apple Cranberry Crumble, 164
Cranberry Coconut Bars, 140

Oats (continued)
Gingery Oat and Molasses
Cookies, 110
Honey Nut Granola Bars, 156
Oat and Whole Wheat
Scones, 92
Oat Apricot Snack Cake, 8
Oat Streusel, 59
PB and J Thumbprint Cookies,
114
Plum Rhubarb Crumble, 174
Praline Topping, 57
Shortbread Turtle Cookie
Bars, 146
Three-Grain Bread, 80
Oat Streusel, 59

P
Pastry Dough
Double-Crust Pie Pastry, 54
Pie Pastry, 48
Single-Crust Pie Pastry, 58
PB and J Thumbprint Cookies, 114
Peanut Butter
PB and J Thumbprint Cookies,
114
Peanut Butter Bran Muffins,
86
Peanut Butter Cupcakes, 30
Peanut Buttery Frosting, 30
Peanutty Double Chip
Cookies, 106
Perfect Peanut Butter
Pudding, 186
Peanut Butter Bran Muffins, 86
Peanut Butter Cupcakes, 30
Peanut Buttery Frosting, 30
Peanuts
Honey Nut Granola Bars, 156
PB and J Thumbprint Cookies,
114
Peanutty Double Chip Cookies,
106
Pear
Ginger Pear Cobbler, 170
Pear Spice Cake, 32
Rustic Cranberry-Pear
Galette, 40

Pear Spice Cake, 32
Pecans
    Bananas Foster Crisp, 166
    Cranberry Brie Bubble Bread, 76
    Cranberry Coconut Bars, 140
    Mocha Cinnamon Blondies, 136
    Praline Topping, 57
    Sweet Potato Pecan Pie, 37
    Toffee Cake with Whiskey Sauce, 20
    Turtle Cheesecake, 10
Perfect Peanut Butter Pudding, 186
Pie Pastry, 48
Pies
    Classic Apple Pie, 52
    Coconut Meringue Pie, 62
    Lattice-Topped Cherry Pie, 48
    Plum Walnut Pie, 58
    Strawberry Rhubarb Pie, 54
    Swedish Apple Pie, 44
    Sweet Potato Pecan Pie, 37
Plum
    Plum Rhubarb Crumble, 174
    Plum Walnut Pie, 58
Plum Rhubarb Crumble, 174
Plum Walnut Pie, 58
Praline Pumpkin Tart, 56
Praline Topping, 57
Puddings
    Dark Chocolate Raspberry Bread Pudding, 182
    Perfect Peanut Butter Pudding, 186
    Pumpkin Bread Pudding, 162
Pumpkin
    Praline Pumpkin Tart, 56
    Pumpkin Bread Pudding, 162
    Pumpkin Cheesecake, 28
    Pumpkin Cheesecake Bars, 132
    Pumpkin Cinnamon Rolls, 82
    Pumpkin Streusel Coffeecake, 5
    Pumpkin Swirl Brownies, 138
    Pumpkin Whoopie Minis, 126
    Whole Wheat Pumpkin Bars, 154

Pumpkin Bread Pudding, 162
Pumpkin Cheesecake, 28
Pumpkin Cheesecake Bars, 132
Pumpkin Cinnamon Rolls, 82
Pumpkin Streusel Coffeecake, 5
Pumpkin Swirl Brownies, 138
Pumpkin Whoopie Minis, 126

R
Raspberry
    Dark Chocolate Raspberry Bread Pudding, 182
    Raspberry Macarons, 118
Raspberry Macarons, 118
Red Velvet Cake, 18
Refrigerator Cookies, 104
Rhubarb
    Plum Rhubarb Crumble, 174
    Strawberry Rhubarb Pie, 54
Rich Cocoa Brownies, 130
Rustic Cranberry-Pear Galette, 40

S
Seven Layer Bars, 134
Shortbread Turtle Cookie Bars, 146
Simple Golden Cornbread, 65
Single-Crust Pie Pastry, 58
Snickerdoodles, 100
Strawberry Rhubarb Pie, 54
Swedish Apple Pie, 44
Sweet Potato Coconut Bars, 144
Sweet Potatoes
    Chocolate Sheet Cake, 16
    Sweet Potato Coconut Bars, 144
    Sweet Potato Pecan Pie, 37
Sweet Potato Pecan Pie, 37

T
Tarts
    Bittersweet Chocolate Tarts, 38
    Chocolate Walnut Toffee Tart, 50

Tarts (continued)
    Lemon Tart, 42
    Praline Pumpkin Tart, 56
    Rustic Cranberry-Pear Galette, 40
    Very Berry Tart, 46
    Warm Apple Crostata, 60
Three-Grain Bread, 80
Toffee Cake with Whiskey Sauce, 20
Toffee Latte Nut Bars, 148
Treacle Bread (Brown Soda Bread), 72
Turtle Cheesecake, 10

V
Very Berry Tart, 46

W
Walnuts
    Apple Cranberry Crumble, 164
    Baklava, 168
    Carrot Cake, 26
    Chocolate Walnut Toffee Tart, 50
    Crumb Topping, 24
    Date-Nut Banana Braid, 74
    Gingery Oat and Molasses Cookies, 110
    Glazed Applesauce Spice Cake, 22
    Pear Spice Cake, 32
    Plum Walnut Pie, 58
    Pumpkin Streusel Coffeecake, 5
    Sweet Potato Coconut Bars, 144
    Toffee Latte Nut Bars, 148
Warm Apple Crostata, 60
White Chocolate
    Butterscotch Malt Zucchini Cake, 14
    Red Velvet Cake, 18
    Shortbread Turtle Cookie Bars, 146
    Whole Wheat Pumpkin Bars, 154

Metric Conversion Chart

VOLUME MEASUREMENTS (dry)

$1/8$ teaspoon = 0.5 mL
$1/4$ teaspoon = 1 mL
$1/2$ teaspoon = 2 mL
$3/4$ teaspoon = 4 mL
1 teaspoon = 5 mL
1 tablespoon = 15 mL
2 tablespoons = 30 mL
$1/4$ cup = 60 mL
$1/3$ cup = 75 mL
$1/2$ cup = 125 mL
$2/3$ cup = 150 mL
$3/4$ cup = 175 mL
1 cup = 250 mL
2 cups = 1 pint = 500 mL
3 cups = 750 mL
4 cups = 1 quart = 1 L

VOLUME MEASUREMENTS (fluid)

1 fluid ounce (2 tablespoons) = 30 mL
4 fluid ounces ($1/2$ cup) = 125 mL
8 fluid ounces (1 cup) = 250 mL
12 fluid ounces ($1 1/2$ cups) = 375 mL
16 fluid ounces (2 cups) = 500 mL

WEIGHTS (mass)

$1/2$ ounce = 15 g
1 ounce = 30 g
3 ounces = 90 g
4 ounces = 120 g
8 ounces = 225 g
10 ounces = 285 g
12 ounces = 360 g
16 ounces = 1 pound = 450 g

DIMENSIONS

$1/16$ inch = 2 mm
$1/8$ inch = 3 mm
$1/4$ inch = 6 mm
$1/2$ inch = 1.5 cm
$3/4$ inch = 2 cm
1 inch = 2.5 cm

OVEN TEMPERATURES

250°F = 120°C
275°F = 140°C
300°F = 150°C
325°F = 160°C
350°F = 180°C
375°F = 190°C
400°F = 200°C
425°F = 220°C
450°F = 230°C

BAKING PAN SIZES

Utensil	Size in Inches/Quarts	Metric Volume	Size in Centimeters
Baking or	$8 \times 8 \times 2$	2 L	$20 \times 20 \times 5$
Cake Pan	$9 \times 9 \times 2$	2.5 L	$23 \times 23 \times 5$
(square or	$12 \times 8 \times 2$	3 L	$30 \times 20 \times 5$
rectangular)	$13 \times 9 \times 2$	3.5 L	$33 \times 23 \times 5$
Loaf Pan	$8 \times 4 \times 3$	1.5 L	$20 \times 10 \times 7$
	$9 \times 5 \times 3$	2 L	$23 \times 13 \times 7$
Round Layer	$8 \times 1 1/2$	1.2 L	20×4
Cake Pan	$9 \times 1 1/2$	1.5 L	23×4
Pie Plate	$8 \times 1 1/4$	750 mL	20×3
	$9 \times 1 1/4$	1 L	23×3
Baking Dish	1 quart	1 L	—
or Casserole	$1 1/2$ quart	1.5 L	—
	2 quart	2 L	—